Better

God's Plan > My Plan

Jason Hanash

Sermon To Book
www.sermontobook.com

Better / Jason Hanash
ISBN: 978-1-945793-83-7

*Dedicated to the life-giving church I have the joy and
privilege of pastoring—
Discovery Church in Bakersfield, CA*

CONTENTS

Made for More

What things have you spent your life pursuing more of? Has the acquisition of more or better things left you feeling full, or does emptiness remain?

My Honda Accord was a very reliable car, but it eventually started falling apart, as all material things do. I remember telling a friend, who happened to be a car salesman, about the problems it was giving me. He had the solution for me. He said, "It's time for an upgrade! I can see you in an Audi!" I said, "Sure, if you're buying!" An Audi wouldn't make things better—it would make me broke.

How many times do we strive for things that we think will make our lives better, but instead they only leave us broken? We can, of course, be financially broke, but we can also find ourselves broken relationally, spiritually, emotionally, or mentally; things that had the promise of making our lives better failed to deliver. I want to help you see that money, career, relationships, success, and power don't always make our situations better.

The devil is crafty; the Bible says he schemes. We take his bait as a surefire way for improvement, but we are ultimately left broken. Better always comes with a price tag. And sometimes, we honestly look at the price of the bait, and we knowingly say, "Okay, I'll pay that." "I'll sacrifice my family for my career." "I'll sacrifice my health and my long-term peace for an evening to drink it away."

There's always a price.

That's what happens when we fall for the myth of more. In this book, I hope to show you how much better God's plan is than the plan you might be living, but I want to show that you were actually made for more.

Now to him who is able to do immeasurably more than all we ask or imagine, according to his power that is at work within us, to him be glory in the church and in Christ Jesus throughout all generations, for ever and ever! Amen.
—Ephesians 3:20–21

My fear is that we end up in ordinary living—attainable, "I know I can do this," kind of a living.

I want to stir you to live an extraordinary kind of life. I believe God has called you to live an extraordinary life—not because you're extraordinary, but because He is. It's His power at work within you, but we sometimes choose the ordinary life. For some of you, even Christianity has become boring and mundane, and I believe God wants to move you beyond that in Jesus' name.

We are confident that you are meant for better things,

things that come with salvation.

—Hebrews 6:9 *(NLT)*

The better things God has for you in this life are so contrary to the things to which your mind may be drawn. In Proverbs 8:19, God says, "My fruit is better than life"! To truly have better, we must replace the lies we have fallen for with what God says is *better*.

Every person longs for more because we are made for more. It's time to stop settling for less than God's plan and God's best for our lives.

The Bible says God put eternity in the heart of every man (Ecclesiastes 3:11). This is why each person longs for more than the world can offer. A classic Christian quote says there is a "God-shaped void" in the heart of every man.[1] Although many try to fill it with material possessions and pleasures, only God Himself can fill the aching chasm inside.

The fact that you are reading this book is a good sign that you have heard His invitation and have chosen to follow Him. Or maybe, like so many people, you realize that the world's promise of more and better leaves you feeling empty. Here's the truth: God didn't save you just so you could go to heaven. That isn't the only reason He sent His Son. It is not the only reason why Jesus died. And it definitely is not why Jesus has given us the power of the Holy Spirit.

If Jesus' only mission is to get us to heaven, then we would all be in heaven this very moment. If our only purpose in life is to acquire a ticket to heaven the moment we are saved, we would be ushered into glory immediately.

Instead, Christ came not just to give us life, but a more abundant life (John 10:10).

There is more to this life than a ticket to heaven. Following Jesus is more than a one-time decision about who Jesus is and where we will spend eternity. Following Jesus is walking with Him through life; it's the very act of going where He leads.

The question then arises, "Where is God leading *me*?" What are the better things that God offers? Although every individual's journey is different, and God's plan for our lives is unique, every child of God was created to do three things:

1. Love God,

2. Love each other

3. Change the world.

Your unique purpose will never be realized until you start doing what God has already called you to do. I promise you this—the life God has planned for you is better than the life you have planned for yourself.

A Better Life

Better is one day in your courts than a thousand elsewhere. I would rather be a doorkeeper in the house of my God than dwell in the tents of the wicked.
—Psalm 84:10

So many people simply don't believe a lowly position

in heaven is better than a high place among the wicked. In fact, I didn't believe it for years. Before I was a Christian, I thought Christians had nothing to offer me. To me, Christians were giving up the better life (parties, sex, drugs, and fun) for a lesser life (church, religion, and fuddy-duddy stuff).

You may ask, "How is a life with Christ better than a life without?"

Following Jesus will make your life better and will make you better at life. Because of Jesus, I can forgive freely and I can love greatly. I have more peace, more power, and more purpose.

One day with God is better than a thousand elsewhere. It's better because God's ways are higher than our ways (Isaiah 55:9). Scripture says His love is better than life (Psalm 63:3). A day with God is better than anything the world has to offer. Why?

A day with God is better because with Christ you have the forgiveness of your sins. Your sins have been separated in God's eyes as far as the east is from the west, and He never holds them against you again (Psalm 103:12). A day with God is better because you have the security of knowing that you are in the family of God.

A day with God is better because you have joy unspeakable. Your happiness is not based on the happenings of this world, but you have a joy based on who God is.

A day with God is better because no matter what's going on in your life, you can have a supernatural peace that goes beyond the ability to understand (Philippians 4:7). A day with God is better because you have His divine calling and purpose in your life. When you wake up in the morning, you know that your God knew you before you were ever even born. He knew you in your mother's womb (Psalm 139:13). All of the days of your life were ordained and written in His Book before even one of them came to be (Psalm 139:16). You have a unique calling, purpose, and contribution to make in this life, and that should make your day better!

A day with God's power is better because you have His power. If you're a Christian, the same Spirit that raised Christ from the dead lives inside you (Romans 8:11), and you have access to the very throne room of God (Hebrews 4:16).

A day with God is better because you have His provision. You have everything that you need to do what God wants you to do. Scripture says you have everything you need for life and godliness (2 Peter 1:3).

Now, I hope you hear me clearly—I'm not saying that life will always be easy and that you will never have trials. That's simply not true. When we cling to Jesus during our storms, Jesus is our peace.

Jesus was the disciples' peace in the midst of a literal storm they encountered while crossing the Sea of Galilee. While Jesus slept, a storm threatened to overturn the boat. When awakened by the scared disciples, He was angry at their lack of faith. "You of little faith, why are you so afraid?" (Matthew 8:26). He rebuked the winds, and the storm immediately calmed (Matthew 8:23–27). The disciples had nothing to be afraid of—the storm wasn't a surprise to Jesus, and they, more than anybody, should have trusted in His power.

I want to be close to Jesus and His power. In fact, I'd

rather be in the boat in a storm with Jesus than on the shore without Him, because a day with Him is better than a thousand elsewhere.

What Matters Most?

We spend our lives chasing lesser things when God has better things in store for us.

> *So be careful how you live. Don't live like fools, but like those who are wise. Make the most of every opportunity in these evil days. Don't act thoughtlessly, but understand what the Lord wants you to do.*
> **—Ephesians 5:15–17** *(NLT)*

For you to obtain the better life, you need to start with having the right values. Know what matters most. I believe that we spend the vast majority of our time, energy, money, efforts, worries, concerns, and prayers on things that really, at the end of the day, don't matter!

We can reach for things our entire lives—possessions, accomplishments, status, beauty, etc.—and never realize we were reaching for the wrong things. A commitment to the wrong goals will create the illusion of progress, but it won't bring the reward of fulfillment. We have to discover and determine what really matters in life and align our goals with those values.

I would submit to you that there are only three things that matter in life:

1. God Matters (Love God)

I am sure everyone who has ever heard the phrase "God matters" thinks to themselves, "Amen! Of course God matters!"

But do our lives really reflect that He matters? Could I follow you around and see that God is important to you and that you don't just compartmentalize God to fit into certain portions of your life?

The truth is every one of us is going to stand before Almighty God, the Creator of the universe. And the determining factor of our entering heaven is not going to be our church attendance—not even our good deeds can get us into heaven. As we stand before God, He's going to ask, "Did My Son matter to you? Were you in a relationship with Jesus?"

Matthew 6:33 is a promise to us: "But seek first his kingdom and his righteousness, and all these things will be given to you as well." Above all, you need to put all of your energy, effort, time, thoughts, love, and passion toward your relationship with God. I guarantee—and far better, the Bible guarantees—you'll be glad you did.

Twice, Jesus warns against those who will one day stand before God in heaven with all kinds of reasons why they should be allowed to enter. His response to them won't be, "You didn't do enough good deeds," or "You didn't witness enough," or "You didn't attend church enough," or "You didn't give enough." To those who didn't have a relationship with Jesus, He will say: "I can't let you in. I never *knew* you" (Matthew 7:23, 25:12).

Your relationship with God is everything. But my

dream, my real goal, for me and for you, is to make knowing and serving God so attractive that it literally becomes the highlight of our lives—because God matters. Nothing is better than Him. Here's how Paul says it:

> *But whatever were gains to me I now consider loss for the sake of Christ. What is more, I consider everything a loss because of the surpassing worth of knowing Christ Jesus my Lord, for whose sake I have lost all things. I consider them garbage, that I may gain Christ...*
> **—Philippians 3:7–8**

Christ was Paul's priority. What was once valuable, more, or better in his life, was no longer meaningful.

There is going to be a gravitational pull for every one of us toward things that don't matter, causing us to worship things instead of God. Worship is just love expressed. And at the end of it all, many people are going to wish they didn't put that much love and passion into things that, comparatively, are rubbish.

Jesus told stories about people who put all their energy and passions into things. In the parable of the rich fool, He speaks of a man who spent his life becoming wealthy and searching for self-centered thrills before being condemned by God, which serves as a powerful warning for us:

> *But God said to him, "You fool! This very night your life will be demanded from you. Then who will get what you have prepared for yourself?"*
>
> *This is how it will be with anyone who stores up things for*

himself but is not rich toward God.

—Luke 12:20–21

2. People Matter (Love People)

Do you know why I like teaching that people matter? Because if there's one reason you're upset today, it's most likely due to somebody else. It's very easy in this life to get upset at someone.

Some of you are carrying around offenses and wounds caused by others, and it's destroying your life. It's time to let go. Some of you with deep hurts caused by tremendous offenses, may feel that I don't understand your pain or that I'm trivializing your situation. I do not know the details of your particular situation, but I've seen and counseled many people in my years of being a pastor and there is not an offense that exists that is worth the pain and anger that you are holding on to. Unforgiveness is like drinking poison and then waiting for the other person to die; it will kill you.

I'm here to remind you that people matter to God and they need to matter to you too. God loves us and forgives us; we are called to love others and forgive them, regardless if they deserve it. Forgiveness is a key element in your relationship with others, and ultimately, with God. When you can't forgive others, you're undermining anything better God might have to offer, by replacing joy with bitterness.

People and relationships matter in a world where there are very few things that really matter. In Galatians, Paul says:

*...rather, serve one another humbly in love. For the entire
law is fulfilled in keeping this one command: "Love your
neighbor as yourself." If you bite and devour each other,
watch out or you will be destroyed by each other.*
—Galatians 5:13b–15

Paul's warns that we've forgotten relationships. Our
nation has various tributes every anniversary of 9/11, in-
cluding different television specials and documentaries,
where we see how much people matter. I saw one recently
in which someone who was facing death left a voicemail:
"Honey, I know we fought this morning, but I just want
you to know I love you." In the last moments, the most
important thought was about the people—the relationships.

Psalm 90 tells us God brought forth the whole world,
from everlasting to everlasting (Psalm 90:1–2), that a
thousand years are like a day in His sight (Psalm 90:4),
and that our days pass quickly (Psalm 90:10). Verse 12
says, "Teach us to number our days, that we may gain a
heart of wisdom."

All of a sudden, as I watched those 9/11 documentaries, I realized how few my days are. I started living with
a heart of wisdom. When I think I've got plenty of days,
then I have plenty of time to hold a grudge and be angry.
But it makes it easier to live in peace when we realize that
our days are numbered. Relationships matter, and we need
to value each day with the people we love. You may need
to call someone today and tell that person you love him or
her. Why? Because our time is short, and we need to gain
a heart of wisdom. People matter. You already know it,
but you just need to live as if it's the last day of your life.

We spend too much time fighting with people, fussing with people, and getting mad at people when we're supposed to be spending our time impacting people, loving people, and serving people. Your life is really about the difference you can make in people's lives.

Does it really matter that much? This is what Jesus said:

> *For I was hungry and you gave me something to eat, I was thirsty and you gave me something to drink....*
>
> *...whatever you did for one of the least of these brothers of mine, you did for me.*
> **—Matthew 25:35a, 40b**

Jesus said, when you do it to them, you're doing it unto Him. At the end of the day, God matters! People matter!

3. Eternity Matters (Change the World)

Did you know that the vast majority of your life will be spent on the other side of death? Thank God for that, by the way. That's what sometimes keeps me going through my rough days. When I speak to those who experience the death of a loved one, I am sad for them as they grieve, but I am reminded that I am grateful for heaven. I thank God that one day, for those who have accepted Christ as their Savior, we will all see Him face to face (1 Corinthians 13:12) and be reunited with believers we love on the other side.

There's coming a day when there'll be no more crying,

sighing, dying, no more insurance, no more tax returns, and no more traffic. The hot light at Krispy Kreme will always be on. Heaven is going to be glorious and exceedingly better than earth (Revelation 21:4). If we are at odds with our loved ones while we're here on earth, we can't show them the love of God. For those who may not know the Lord, this could change eternity for them. Eternity matters. This life is just a vapor, a mist (James 4:14). Jesus tells us that what we store up during this temporary life doesn't matter:

Watch out! Be on your guard against all kinds of greed; a man's life does not consist in an abundance of possessions.
—Luke 12:15

Do not store up for yourselves treasures on earth, where moth and rust destroy, and where thieves break in and steal. But store up for yourselves treasures in heaven, where moth and rust do not destroy, and where thieves do not break in and steal. For where your treasure is, there your heart will be also.
—Matthew 6:19–21

Put your treasures toward the proper priorities and know what matters: people, relationships, and eternity!

You were made for more, but not the world's version of more. In this book, I want to help you discover what that is, so that you can come to the conclusion I have: God's plan is better than our plans.

Practical Application

What does it mean to live a life that's made for more? This book will help you answer that question and apply it to your life. At the end of each chapter, workbook sections will give you practical tools to live a life that is *better*.

When you are home with two kids and living in the daily chaos of dirty diapers and spilled milk, remember that these relationships are a tiny portion of eternity. When you grind through a day job to make ends meet, keep in mind that the connections you make with your colleagues have eternal values. There's always more to your circumstances than you see. Do you live as if people and your eternity are in view?

When I live with these values—the truths that God matters, people matter, and eternity matters—I'm able to live an unstoppable life. Whether you're living in a season of harvest or a season of drought, focusing on these values helps you experience a life that's made for more.

WORKBOOK

Introduction Questions

Question: What are some things you have spent your life pursuing more of? Has the acquisition of more or better in these areas left you feeling satisfied or unsatisfied? If you could have more of any one thing right now, what would it be?

_____

_____

_____

_____

_____

_____

_____

_____

_____

_____

_____

Question: The life God has planned for you is better than the life you have planned for yourself. Describe the life that you would plan for yourself if you could control your own destiny. Does entrusting your future entirely to God fill you with peace or with apprehension? Are there reasons you doubt that His is better than your own?

_____

_____

_____

_____

_____

_____

_____

_____

_____

_____

_____

_____

Question: God matters, people matter, and eternity matters. If someone were to examine your life from the past week, how would they see these priorities displayed? Would it be obvious that these are the three most important things to you? In what ways are you investing in each of these areas?

_____

_____

_____

_____

_____

_____

_____

_____

_____

_____

Action: Make a list of all of the things that you might do in a typical week. Include mundane activities, such as grocery shopping, paying bills, or walking the dog. Next to each item on your list, write down a way that you can do that activity with more meaning and purpose. How can you use that part of your life to intentionally glorify God, to specifically invest in relationships with others, or to impact eternity in some small but definitive way?

Introduction Notes

_____

_____

_____

_____

_____

_____

_____

_____

_____

_____

_____

_____

_____

_____

_____

_____

_____

_____

_____

_____

_____

_____

_____

CHAPTER ONE

Living for God in an Ungodly World

We live in a world gone haywire. Our moral fabric seems to be decaying at breakneck speed. Things that were once considered shamefully hidden are now publicly celebrated. The previously unimaginable has become commonplace. In just a few short decades, our culture's response to Bible-believing Christians has gone from grudging respect, to a patronizing pat on the head and a bit of indifference, to outright hostility. It's mind-boggling, even frightening.

Yet, as pastor and author Chris Hodges explains in *The Daniel Dilemma*, the Bible holds the answer to living as a Christian in an anti-Christian culture.[2]

Daniel and Worldly Culture

Daniel bravely managed his confusion and fear while living for God in an ungodly world. He found a way, in a culture far more wicked than anything we face, to glorify and serve God with such integrity and power that kings, servants, and an entire nation turned to acknowledge the one true God.

If you are not familiar with the Bible or the book of Daniel, let me give you some background.[3] Daniel would have lived somewhere around the year 600 BC during the time when King Nebuchadnezzar of Babylon, which is located in modern-day Iraq, defeated Israel. Israel's defeat was prophesied to take place because of their continued disobedience to God (Jeremiah 25).

During this captivity, or exile, Israel was taken away as slaves, and many who didn't die in the war were brought into Babylon. Daniel was a part of the group that was taken in captivity to Babylon.

The interesting part of the book is that there's a constant confrontation between Daniel and the worldly, Babylonian culture. Daniel and his company were godly and were trying to obey God, but the law of the land was asking them to live against God's commands and compromise their convictions.

In the third year of the reign of Jehoiakim king of Judah, Nebuchadnezzar king of Babylon came to Jerusalem and besieged it. And the LORD delivered Jehoiakim king of Judah into his hand, along with some of the articles from the temple of God. These he carried off to the temple of his god in Babylonia and put in the treasure house of his god.

Then the king ordered Ashpenaz, chief of his court officials, to bring into the king's service some of the Israelites from the royal family and the nobility—young men without any physical defect, handsome, showing aptitude for every kind of learning, well informed, quick to understand, and qualified to serve in the king's palace. He was to teach them the language and literature of the Babylonians. The king assigned them a daily amount of food and wine from the king's table. They were to be trained for three years, and after that they were to enter the king's service.

Among those who were chosen were some from Judah: Daniel, Hananiah, Mishael and Azariah.
—Daniel 1:1–6

According to Jewish dietary laws, Daniel, Hananiah, Mishael, and Azariah were not allowed to eat much of the food the Babylonians offered. And, they were asked to worship false gods, as the Babylonian culture did. The young men were confronted with a culture asking them to do things they did not want to, and shouldn't, do.

So, the question turns toward us. What do you do when the culture shifts? When the culture turns from God, do you shift, too? Although culture changes, God never changes.

Don't become so well-adjusted to your culture that you fit into it without even thinking.
—Romans 12:2 *(MSG)*

You were made for more than this world can offer. God has something better in store for you! But if you want to live for God and live a better life, you must follow God's purposes, and not the world's cultural practices.

The culture will shift, tempting you to change with it and draw you away from God. Are we going to change with culture and then ask God to change?

The Culture Will Try to Rename You

The culture is going to try to change you from knowing your identity is in Christ into finding your identity in the world. This identity crisis is a direct assault on your God-given destiny. If you give in to the culture, you are at risk of living with a label the world puts on you, rather than the label God puts on you.

> *The chief official gave them new names: to Daniel, the name Belteshazzar; to Hananiah, Shadrach; to Mishael, Meshach; and to Azariah, Abednego.*
> **—Daniel 1:7**

This is the first thing that the enemy, and the culture, will try to do to you: change your name, or your identity. Let's look at the meaning of these names.

Daniel's name means "God is my judge."[4] They renamed him Belteshazzar, which means, "Bel, protect his life."[5] The meaning of the name Daniel turned attention to God—to whom Daniel is answerable—while the name Belteshazzar pointed elsewhere, to a false god and a king at the center of the culture in that time and place. When focus on the culture replaces focus on God, however, it doesn't mean God will stop judging man.

The enemy tries to put the focus from God to man by suggesting to us, "Don't listen to God. God doesn't have the right name for you. Man does. That's who you really are." And I will say to you, don't listen to what the world's labels are—listen to God!

Hananiah means "God has favored."[6] However, the

world couldn't leave him with such a God-honoring name. Instead, they gave him the Babylonian name *Shadrach*, which means, "I am fearful of God."[7] The culture was saying, "You need to be afraid of God. God's not good—He's mad at you." The narrative in today's has gone from "God is good" to "God is bad."

The world tells us that serving God will restrict us and make us outcasts. The Bible's instructions telling us 'thou shalt not' (Exodus 20 KJV) must mean God is against us, right? But it's a lie! Everything God has written for you is for your good (Jeremiah 29:11). And if you follow His ways, you'll live a life of fulfillment and joy in your relationship with Him. God is not bad. He is a gracious, loving, awesome God. It's an incredible honor to serve and praise our God.

The name *Mishael* means "Who is what God is?"[8] Basically it means, "there is no one like my God." What an awesome name! But the Babylonians changed it to *Meshach*, which means, "I am despised, contemptible, and humiliated."[9] The Babylonians wanted him to hush, as the world today wants of us Christians need to hush, take our business elsewhere, stop having principles and convictions.

After feeling ostracized, it's easy for us to hide in our church services and be scared to outwardly express our faith. The enemy is trying to make cowards out of Christians in our current culture, but we must have confidence in being children of the one and only God, rather than despised, contemptible, and humiliated, as in Meshach's name. Don't be afraid to say a prayer of thanks at a restaurant. Don't be afraid to side with God's Word in a conversation. Don't be afraid to live what you believe.

And as we live out our faith, loving God and others, we want to show the world that there is no one like our God. The final Jewish name was *Azariah*, meaning "Yahweh has helped [me]."[10]

Yahweh is an endearing term. It's personal, saying to the believer, "I am close to God, I know God, and God is personally involved in my life, to the degree that He has helped me." This young man's name was changed to *Abednego*, which means "servant of Nebo."[11]

The name change signifies the Babylonians ultimate goal—to draw them away from serving God and to change their identities from being children of God to being slaves to the world. Sound reminiscent of our culture today?

When culture shifts, you better know who you are.

How do you know who you are? You need to be secure in your identity in Christ. We are bombarded with the lies of our culture, which rob us of our God-given identities and God-given purposes. However, you were not meant to do this alone. God created a church, a people to walk the truth out with you. Many churches use small groups, close settings where you can talk and see the world for what it is. You need to let God draw you close, and you need to find your redemptive calling among believers and the church, so you can do something great for God. He has great things in store for every one of us.

The Culture Will Try to Tame You

The world's culture is trying to make us into a group of people who don't live with conviction and who have no principles or faith. It's trying to lure you into something that you know is wrong. You may be tempted to conform to the world's standards, but stand strong as Daniel did:

> *But Daniel resolved not to defile himself with the royal food and wine, and he asked the chief official for permission not to defile himself this way.*
> **—Daniel 1:8**

I love how Daniel never attacked the culture around him. He never shouted, "You're all wrong! You're going to hell!" Instead, he just resolved within himself, "The world can go against God, but I choose differently." He "resolved not to defile himself" (Daniel 1:8).

The culture will constantly try to tame you. To control you. To make you less threatening. To not speak up when someone is bullied. To ignore the poor. To go places that will tempt you to sin.

But stand firm in your desire to live a righteous life and live with true joy and true fulfillment. To live close to Him is to be wild and untamed—uncontrolled by the culture. You don't need me to tell you the specifics of how to do that, because you have the Holy Spirit as your guide (John 16:13).

When culture shifts, don't lose your convictions. You have the Holy Spirit and God's Word, so let the Holy Spirit speak to you about what's right and what's not right and follow God—indeed, most of all follow God and do what the Lord shows you!

The Culture Will Try to Claim You

There is a battle going on for you right now. Whom will you follow? Whom will you serve? Let's pick up in the book of Daniel again:

> *Daniel then said to the guard whom the chief official had appointed over Daniel, Hananiah, Mishael and Azariah, "Please test your servants for ten days: Give us nothing but vegetables to eat and water to drink. Then compare our appearance with that of the young men who eat the royal food, and treat your servants in accordance with what you see." So he agreed to this and tested them for ten days.*
> **—Daniel 1:11–14**

There will always be a test, moment of pressure, or defining moment. Sometimes it will be the Holy Spirit telling you to stop, but sometimes there will be a moment when culture will get in your face and try to sway you, like Daniel and the forbidden foods, but you have to stay strong and say, "I won't do it," or "I'm not going into that building," or "I'm not watching that movie," or "I'm not saying yes to that."

There is a battle going on for you right now, whether you are young or old, new Christian or mature believer, there's a battle raging for you. The world is pulling you on one arm; you feel the tug. And God is pulling another way, and you get to cast the deciding vote—will I live for God in an ungodly world? There will always be a moment when your faith will be tested.

I remember when I fully gave my life to Christ and completely surrendered when I was twenty years old. I had known God and even claimed to be a Christian before that, but I wasn't living for Him.

After I became a Christian and started changing some of my behaviors, my friends would still try to get me to go out and drink and smoke pot with them. I vividly remember having a conversation with one friend about beer and weed, both mind-altering substances the Holy Spirit had convicted me were not to be part of my life. I was to be sober-minded (1 Peter 5:8). My friend tried to convince me that these things weren't bad for me or that they weren't evil substances. He lobbied that we wouldn't be causing trouble or hurting anyone, even though we were underage. My friend felt as though I was judging him by refusing to do the things I used to do. And I felt both the pull toward the world and the pull toward God.

You know what I'm talking about, even if you didn't party as a kid. Perhaps it is certain kinds of movies or music. Or the kinds of friends you hang around. We all have certain temptations, and God wants better for us.

At that moment, I was standing on an edge. Leading up to that moment, combined with what my friend was telling me, I wondered, "What is going to be the direction of my life?" I could choose one way or the other. And I chose Christ. And like me, you will always be tested.

When culture shifts, as with my friends, never give in to the pressure.

"Come on, let's go, your mom won't find out." "Come on, let's take these supplies from work." ""You should drink this." "You should try that." "You should look at this." "You should click on that." "Go ahead and cheat on your spouse—what they don't know won't hurt them."

No. Just no.

You will be tested. That's why I'm urging you, if you want to be a difference maker, never give in to the pressure. Daniel 1:15–20 says:

> *At the end of the ten days they looked healthier and better nourished than any of the young men who ate the royal food. So the guard took away their choice food and the wine they were to drink and gave them vegetables instead.*
>
> *To these four young men God gave knowledge and understanding of all kinds of literature and learning. And Daniel could understand visions and dreams of all kinds.*
>
> *At the end of the time set by the king to bring them into his service, the chief official presented them to Nebuchadnezzar. The king talked with them, and he found none equal to Daniel, Hananiah, Mishael and Azariah; so they entered the king's service. In every matter of wisdom and understanding about which the king questioned them, he found them ten times better than all the magicians and enchanters in his whole kingdom.*

I'm here to declare to the world that our God is ten times better than anything the world can ever offer you! God is ten times better! God is better!

Practical Application

I have two questions for you to ask yourself and ponder, and I'm asking them to stir you toward your own response before God and to what the Holy Spirit has been saying to you.

First: Will you change the world, or will the world

change you? You have to decide—when the culture shifts, will you? You have to know what you'll do before you're tempted. And you must decide whether we're going to set the culture or reflect the culture. I would say to you, let's be a people of God who don't get in people's faces, posting on social media of everyone and everything we're against—don't go there. That's not the example Daniel set for us.

And on the other hand, we don't have to look like everybody else. We don't need to reflect the culture—we need to set the culture. We don't need to be a thermometer—we need to be a thermostat.

Jesus said to let your light shine in front of men, that they may see your good works (Matthew 5:16). The world should notice something different in your life. The love for your enemies, the joy in the midst of storms, the principles you live by—it's Jesus. Jesus said your life should cause others to glorify your God in heaven (Matthew 5:16). Will you change the world, or will the world change you?

Here's the second question: Will your identity come from God or will it come from the world? When people look at you, will they see Jesus, or will they see the world?

> ...and he has identified us as his own by placing the Holy Spirit in our hearts...
> **—2 Corinthians 1:22** (NLT)

To have an identity that reflects Jesus, you must abandon any image of yourself that is not from God. You must stop accepting what others have said about you, how others have labeled you, and how others have defined you. Abandon what the culture and this world say about you.

Instead start believing what God says about you. He is pleased with how He created you. Believe that God defines you, not our culture!

Do not be defined by your feelings. Do not be defined by the opinions of others or by your circumstances. You're not defined by your successes or failures. You're not defined by the car you drive, the amount of money you make, or the house you say you own (when the bank really does).

You are defined by God and God alone. He identifies you as His own. You were made for more than this world can offer. You were made for better. You were made to love God, love each other, and change the world.

Spend time with God's people. You are not meant to do this alone. Those connected with Christ will tell you what you need to know about yourself.

WORKBOOK

Chapter One Questions

Question: What are some current cultural trends that concern you? In what ways do you see the culture becoming increasingly hostile toward Christianity? Describe some good and bad responses to this hostility that you have observed from believers.

_____

_____

_____

_____

_____

_____

_____

_____

_____

_____

_____

Question: How can you stand up against the wrongs that you see in the culture without attacking the people who are doing those wrongs? Give an example of standing for truth in a loving way. Do you tend to focus more on love or truth, and how can you do a better job of incorporating both into your life with balance and integrity?

_____

_____

_____

_____

_____

_____

_____

_____

_____

_____

_____

Question: When have you faced a defining test about who would claim you—Christ or the culture? How did you respond? Have you made the decision to choose Christ over the world, or are you still trying to let both have a claim on you? Why is it impossible to follow both?

_____

_____

_____

_____

_____

_____

_____

_____

_____

_____

_____

Action: When culture shifts, you better know who you are. Make a list from the Bible of who God says you are when your identity is in Christ. The following passages will get you started: Ephesians 1; 1 Peter 2; and Romans 8.

Chapter One Notes

CHAPTER TWO

Focusing on Relationship over Religion

When we talk about loving God, what appears in your mind?

Rules?

Religion?

Reading?

I'm not saying these three areas are inherently bad, but many of us must change how we think about God and salvation.

Salvation is not about simply reading your Bible. It's not a religion, either, in the sense of being about rules, regulations, or rituals. Salvation is about a relationship with God that begins on earth, not in heaven.

Most people start the first moments of their faith by living on fire, being full of love and gaining a fresh start with God. After a short while, however, the human heart pulls toward a religion of rules with lists of dos and don'ts that impress people. We naturally drift away from a relationship with Him.

The apostle Paul, when writing to the church in Galatia, addressed this very problem. He said:

> *I am astonished that you are so quickly deserting the one who called you to live in the **grace** of Christ and are turning to a **different gospel**—which is really no gospel at all. Evidently some people are throwing you into confusion and are trying to pervert the gospel of Christ.*
>
> —***Galatians 1:6–7*** *(emphasis added)*

Grace is the key word here. Paul was saying, "I'm so surprised that after the teaching I gave you and the freedom you found, you have gone right back to a 'different' gospel." Some of you may be wondering, "What gospel is this? Is there more than one?" Yes—there are actually two gospels, or two approaches, to God in this example.

Paul saw that the Galatians had begun preaching a different gospel. He was fed up because Jewish-converted Christians were spreading a belief to new believers that to be "godly," they had to be circumcised.[12] I know that sounds odd in our culture now, but this was a big deal back then. Circumcision was part of Jewish custom.

In Acts 15, there was actually a public debate over this topic. The church leaders were literally debating whether they should require circumcision surgery for new believers.

As believers, we've found grace—this free gift from God, which frees us from the need to be legalistic (Romans 6:23; Ephesians 2:8). But there remains a tendency to go right back into a religious kind of relationship with

God, as the Galatians did, by placing our central focus on pious acts instead of on our relationship with Him, creating a religious gospel instead of a grace-centered gospel.

Most of you reading this book have found Jesus and His grace, but it's human nature to forget what Jesus has done for us and revert back to what we can do for ourselves. We drift away from God's grace and goodness in the gospel, and we turn our relationship into a dead religion.

Here's the key question: how do we have relationship instead of religion?

Religion Versus Relationship

Human thinking drives us toward the desire to accomplish things ourselves, but the Bible teaches something different when it comes to knowing Christ. The message of Christianity can get messed up and perverted, and if we're not careful, we can become like the Galatian church, focusing on what rituals we have to perform and what hoops we have to jump through to have a relationship with God.

Are you pursuing goodness and godliness for your sake, or are you pursuing Jesus?

Let me explain it in a few different ways to make sure you understand the difference between the two choices, religion and relationship.

Religion Focuses on What You Do

The focus of religion is all about you.

For example, if you find that you are merely reading the Bible in order to complete a certain number of chapters, rather than because you love the Word of God, you may be guilty of making your walk with Christ about religion. Thoughts such as, "I used to read five chapters a day, and now I'm up to eight a day, which means I'm becoming a stronger Christian," are an indication that your focus is off.

Check boxes should never be a path for becoming a stronger Christian and growing in your faith.

Relationship Focuses on What Jesus Has Done

When we are in relationship, we're not thinking about how long we prayed, how many hours we served, or how many chapters we read. Our relationship with Jesus isn't based on stats and doesn't involve spiritually sizing up ourselves or others. Do not focus on what you—focus on what Jesus has done. Let me put it this way. If I'm reading my Bible, I'm not focused on how much of it I read. Instead, I'm focused on how much of Jesus I can find in what I've read. My question is not whether I've met a quota, but rather, "Where are You, Lord? If it takes me ten chapters or two, I need to get closer to You."

Some people think they have a corner on the market of God because they have a deep understanding of the Bible. Scripture tells us, however, that head knowledge should not be our focus.

You study the Scriptures diligently because you think that in them you have eternal life. These are the very Scriptures

that testify about me, yet you refuse to come to me to have
life.

—John 5:39–40

You aren't supposed to just read the Bible cover to
cover and memorize a ton of verses. It's good to do, don't
misunderstand me. God wants you to read it and study it
(2 Timothy 2:15). In fact, my church has a school of ministry here where we train people in the Bible, but my goal
is not to offer them knowledge so they're simply brainy
Christians. My goal is to draw them closer to Jesus. I don't
want them to just *read* the Bible—I want them to *experi-*
ence the Bible. I want them to find the person of the Bible,
who is Jesus.

Religion Focuses on Getting God's Approval

Inherently, many believe God is mad at them. Most re-
ligions play on the idea that God must be placated or
pacified, like ancient Greco-Roman gods, which is in contrast with Christ and the Bible, centered on grace and love.

I remember for my first pastoral assignment I inherited
an old desk. I'm convinced this desk had been a part of
the church as far back as Jesus' Sermon on the Mount! In
the desk were piles of old gospel tracts, with illustrations
of God in a massive chair—no face, just a circle—just angry God dishing out punishment like a vengeful being
bent on destruction.

I'm sure these tracts didn't give anybody the right picture of God. The Bible says in Zephaniah 3:17, "The
LORD your God is with you, the Mighty Warrior who

saves. He will take great delight in you." God is in a good mood, not a bad one.

But we often view Him as mad and requiring a lot of hard work from us to win His approval.

Trying to get God's approval is the other gospel. You don't need to get God's approval, and you know why? God already loves you. You need to focus on receiving a love that already exists.

Relationship Focuses on Receiving God's Love

God knows the sin in your life. He's aware of your every thought, every public and secret deed. He knows the foolish decisions you've made, the people you've hurt, and the silly things you wish you could go back and change. He knows all of them (Psalm 139). And yet, He still loves you. Now, He doesn't like what you did, so please don't confuse the idea that His love depends on your actions. He doesn't like the sin, but he *loves you.* He's in love with you. And when you understand His feelings, it changes everything about the way you relate to Him.

In fact, your view of God will determine your relationship with Him. How you see Him will determine how you relate to Him. For example, if you think He's upset with you, here's how it might play out. You did a few things this week that you probably shouldn't have, so you say in your mind, "I'd better not clap too loud today in church, or be too excited about Jesus, because, Lord knows, I'd be acting like a hypocrite." So everything in your heart is drawing you to a closeness to God in worship, and yet you talk yourself out of it because you think He's mad at you. The Scriptures say it this way: "But God demonstrates his own love for us in this: While we were still sinners, Christ died for us" (Romans 5:8).

You don't need to change for God to start loving you. He loves you so that you can change! You don't need to get your act together to grow closer to God. You grow closer to God so you can get your act together.

He wants you to come as close to Him as you can and love Him with all your being. In Him you don't receive condemnation; instead you get the conviction of the Holy Spirit to help you do right. So even though we sin, run to Him in worship and that love will change everything. I love this verse: "We love because he first loved us" (1 John 4:19).

In other words, whatever we do, the reason we worship is because when we were still being idiots, He still loved us.

One of my personal pet peeves is when people talk about serving God like it's a sacrifice. Not me! You're eating from the wrong tree, brothers and sisters! Serving God is the best choice I've made in my life I love Him because He first loved me. And service comes from my love for Him.

Duty Versus Desire

A religious mindset says: "Do it, do it, do it." "You didn't pray enough." "You didn't read enough." "That's not enough." "You may not want to do it, but do it anyway." Religion is too often about trying to be good, despite our sinful hearts, while God hovers overhead with a giant flyswatter ready to smack us when we step out of line.

But the other approach—relationship—says that worshiping God is the joy of our lives. It's not that *we have to* worship God, it's that *we get to* worship God. We get to be in relationship with Him and have Him by our side, walking with us every step of the way.

Let me show you this in the Bible:

> *In fact, this is love for God: to keep his commands. And his commands are not burdensome... Whoever has the Son has life; whoever does not have the Son of God does not have life.*
> **—1 John 5:3, 12**

I must admit, His commands are terribly burdensome if you're not in love with Him. If you're not in love with God, the instructions in the Bible will be the hardest thing you've ever done. If you're in love, it's the greatest joy of your life to do what's written in God's Word. Everything changes because of love.

Practical Application

What are you pursuing in your life? Do you practice a form of godliness just for the sake of checking the right number of boxes off in your religion? Or are you pursuing a relationship with God?

Imagine being in a marriage where your spouse is only interested in marriage, but not interested in you. It would be a lifeless marriage. Contrast that with a marriage in which both spouses cherish, treasure, and value one another. A couple with that kind of love will be happy and stay together for a lifetime.

How do you grow that close to God? First, read your Bible. His words are written for us to see His character and know who He is and what He wants in a relationship. Read to know who He is. And secondly, talk to Him. Pray. Tell Him how you feel and what's happening. And then listen. Prayer is a conversation with God, just like you would have with a friend.

Once the bonds of friendship are tightened, letting your friend down is the last thing you want to do. That's love. That's a relationship. Is God your friend? Or is He simply your religion? Let's look deeper into what that relationship will look like.

WORKBOOK

Chapter Two Questions

Question: What are some things you feel you must *do* to earn or keep God's favor or to be godly? What attitudes do you have about fulfilling these self-imposed religious duties?

_____

_____

_____

_____

_____

_____

_____

_____

_____

_____

Question: Think about the best human relationship in your life. What made it work? What made you and the other person close? What can you learn from this human relationship about how to interact with God relationally?

_____

_____

_____

_____

_____

_____

_____

_____

_____

_____

_____

Question: Do God's commands and the instructions of His Word seem burdensome to you or is obeying God a natural outflow of your love for Him? If you don't have a desire to obey Him or serve Him, what are some things that you can do to pursue a relationship with Him and grow in your love for Him?

_____

_____

_____

_____

_____

_____

_____

_____

_____

_____

_____

_____

Action: What ideas or qualities come to your mind when you think about God? Just as you made a list of how God describes *your* identity, now make a list of God's biblically defined identity. A Bible-based study about the names and/or attributes of God will prove an invaluable help in having a right picture of God in your mind.

Chapter Two Notes

_____

_____

_____

_____

_____

_____

_____

_____

_____

_____

_____

_____

_____

_____

_____

_____

_____

_____

_____

_____

_____

CHAPTER THREE

Building a Relationship with God

God never intended to be your religion. He always wanted to be in a relationship with you. God doesn't want adherents or congregants—He wants *sons* and *daughters*.

> So in Christ Jesus you are all children of God through faith...
>
> **—Galatians 3:26**

He doesn't want sons in the male sense of the word, but children, both male and female, in a spiritual sense. It's one of the mysteries of faith. When we are born again of the Spirit, God literally changes our lives.

> But when the set time had fully come, God sent his Son, born of a woman, born under the law, to redeem those under the law, that we might receive adoption to **sonship**. Because you are his sons, God sent the Spirit of his Son into our hearts, the Spirit who calls out, "Abba, Father." So you are no longer a slave, but God's child; and since you are his

child, God has made you also an heir.
—Galatians 4:4–7 *(emphasis added)*

God sent the Spirit of His Son to live in our hearts. I love that! We're not talking about a belief system, an idea, or a perspective. This is something tangible and transformative that takes place in our hearts.

When we accept Him and the Spirit dwells within us, He says that we won't address God religiously, but rather relationally—calling Him "Abba, Father." Abba, as we'll talk about later, means "Daddy," not just a father figure.

The concept of being a child of God, or in the family of God, was completely foreign to the Galatian church because to them, God was distant. God was in heaven. They thought He would strike them down in a second if they stepped out of line, as Zeus did with a lightning bolt! It's simply how humans like to imagine God.

I believe some of these ideas still carry over into our concept of God. But learn from Paul who essentially said, "Look, this is different. Now you get to cry out, 'Abba, Father!'"

Slaves Versus Sons

I want to make sure you understand the difference between calling God "Abba" and simply calling Him "God," because chances are, some of us are operating in the wrong kind of relationship. We're operating out of a slave kind of relationship and not a son relationship. Let's look at the difference between these two.

The Slave Has a Master

Imagine you are a slave. As with all slaves, you are owned and possessed by someone and have no choices of your own. The master is always mad at you for one reason or another, usually something you didn't quite do to his liking, and the master is always demanding something from you. If you do anything wrong, you're brutally punished, usually in a most humiliating way. So when you approach the master with any request, you fall on your face and beg him to be nice to you.

The slave's mindset is heartbreaking.

Many Christians have a slave mindset toward God. If we see God, we're going to fall on our faces and crawl away. There's a pilgrimage in Mexico for the Virgin of Guadalupe where the people, in a form of penance and to prove that God is feared, kneel and crawl on their knees all the way to church. They are misguided and think that crawling, even to the point that there is no more skin left on their knees, is a form of respect to God. This is *not* the spirit God wants you to have! This is a sad slavery that had engulfed their lives.

The Son Has a Father

A father and child is a different kind of relationship than a master and a slave. When Jesus was on this earth, children listened to His teaching, either sitting close or on His lap so they might be blessed. The Bible says that His disciples were preventing kids from coming to Jesus (Matthew 19:13–14). But Jesus said to let the children come. Jesus was not the serious person that Hollywood always shows Him to be—malnourished, sad, and serious, walking around in His robe, suave and sophisticated. That is not Jesus! I think He must have kept candy in his robe pockets to hand out, or He must have been silly for all of those kids to gravitate toward Him. He was a child magnet!

It's important that you know the difference between a slave and master relationship and a father and child relationship. Look at Romans 8, for the same concept.

> *The Spirit you received does not make you slaves, so that you live in fear again; rather, the Spirit you received brought about your adoption to sonship. And by him we cry, "Abba, Father." The Spirit himself testifies with our spirit that we are God's children.*
> **—Romans 8:15–16**

Names define a relationship. Now, that word "Abba" might not mean much to you, because it's an Aramaic term. That's the term Paul and others would've used in their day for "Daddy," so, it's the most endearing way to talk about your father. We cry, "Abba, Father" (Romans 8:15b).

So, when you pray, how do you talk to God? In what terms? The Bible is saying, "Cry out to Daddy!" I know it makes some of you feel uncomfortable, but God wants the relationship to change to where it's more endearing—from master and slave to father and child.

Some people address me as "Reverend Hanash," which shows they don't know me well. I'm known by people around town as "Pastor Jason" or "Jason" or "PJ." That's a closer relationship, and one I long for.

Someone once asked me, "What do you want me to call you?" I said, "I don't care, just call me whatever makes you comfortable." I don't need a title in front of my name, I just want to be called. I want to be endeared to you.

The way you call someone determines the relationship. I love that! Let's look at the next difference between the slave and child relationship.

The Slave Is an Employee

Have you ever sat down at a restaurant and been able to tell that your server doesn't really have the best interest of the business at heart? They may treat you like you're a problem rather than as a person who is, in actuality, helping to pay their wages. I went to a restaurant recently that was overflowing with customers waiting to be seated, despite a plethora of open tables. The hostess just wasn't in a hurry to get the people seated. I promise you, if she owned the business, she'd have been in a bigger hurry to fill the tables. It's different when you own the business.

Some of us see ourselves as employees of God. You may see yourself as working for God, and it's really not in your heart to do your best. In other words, you don't see Christianity as part of the family business. It changes the relationship completely.

The Son Is an Heir

It *is*, indeed, your business though, but you don't work

for God, you work *with* God! I'm an owner with God. So these aren't the church's chairs, these are your chairs. These aren't the church's drums. They are your drums. It's not just God's mission to reach the lost, it's your mission. I'm convinced that when you start seeing your position as heir as God see it, you'll treat the church differently.

Now, when I'm walking to my car, and I see a piece of paper littering the ground, well, that paper is my responsibility, because it is my church,. And when I see a visitor wandering around, that's my visitor, because this is my house. And so I'm going to go up and say, "Hey, is there something I can help you find?" Do you see the difference?

> *Now if we are children, then we are heirs—heirs of God, and co-heirs with Christ...*
> **—Romans 8:17**

In God's mind, you become a part of everything He has, just as Jesus has. That means that everything Jesus has, God wants you to have. God wants you blessed, so that you can be a blessing to those around you. God wants you healed, so that you can heal those around you. God wants you free, so that you can release those in bondage!

I pray both a personal prayer and a prayer for our church. I ask God to give us more than we need so that we can give away as much of it as we possibly can to change the world—because I'm part of the family business.

The Slave Is Driven by Duty

Following God, for those driven by duty, can become a robotic list of do's and don'ts. You have to go to church. You have to serve. You have to give. While the slave *has to*, the son *gets to*.

Instead of picking up the litter and welcoming the visitor out of duty and grumbling about it, there's a sense of joy in doing things. People watching see you are happy you can make the grounds clean. Visitors see that you honestly appreciate them being there.

A Son Is Driven by Devotion

As a son, my prayer becomes, "I just love You so much, God, that it's my joy to do that for You and with You." Probably the best passage in the Bible that describes the difference between these two motivations is found in Luke 10:

> As Jesus and his disciples were on their way, he came to a village where a woman named Martha opened her home to him. She had a sister called Mary, who sat at the Lord's feet listening to what he said. But Martha was distracted by all the preparations that had to be made. She came to him and asked, "Lord, don't you care that my sister has left me to do the work by myself? Tell her to help me!"
>
> "Martha, Martha," the Lord answered, "you are worried and upset about many things, but few things are needed—or indeed only one. Mary has **chosen** what is **better**..."
>
> **—Luke 10:38–42** *(emphasis added)*

Relationship is better than religion. It's way better! Mary and Martha both loved Jesus, and they both wanted to give to Jesus, but they were doing it with different spirits. Martha chose to serve God through her efforts and her duty—*religion*. Mary chose to serve God through being with Him, delighting in His presence—*relationship*.

Practical Application

Let's go back to Galatians:

> *Formerly, when you did not know God, you were slaves to those who by nature are not gods. But now that you know God—or rather are known by God—how is it that you are turning back to those weak and miserable forces? Do you wish to be enslaved by them all over again?*
> **—Galatians 4:8–9**

Paul corrected the Galatian church, and God is correcting us. What do you have to do then? You have to *know God*. I think there are several steps that, if you put them into practice, will help you know God.

See God as a Father

Start with your eyes. How do you see Him? When you come to God, what does He look like to you? Your view of God will determine your relationship with God.

Ultimately, He is our Father. He's not just any father, either, but one who cares, is with you every step of the way, offering comfort, support, and correction when you need it. So, what does God look like? Let's look at Matthew 7 to explain:

> *Which of you, if your son asks for bread, will give him a stone? Or if he asks for a fish, will give him a snake? If you, then, though you are evil, know how to give good gifts to your children, how much more will your Father in heaven give good gifts to those who ask him!*
> **—Matthew 7:9-11**

Jesus was revolutionizing people's mindsets. He was showing them that God is not a lightning bolt sent to strike down those who displease Him. No! He's a *Father* who wants to give His children good things. He's a pillar leading those who are lost (Exodus 13:21–22).

There's a problem with this, though, because some people have had bad earthly fathers. Sometimes that infects and pollutes their whole view of God. I think the devil uses relationship issues with our fathers to not only drive wedges between our relationships here on earth, but also to also make it more difficult to relate to God the right way.

Approach God Through Relationship, Not Rules

Your approach to God is so critical. Don't approach your prayer life, your word life, your ministry life, or your money, through rules, but instead, approach these facets of your life through relationship.

You study the Scriptures diligently because you think that

> *in them you have eternal life. These are the very Scriptures*
> *that testify about me, yet you refuse to come to me to have*
> *life.*
> **—John 5:39–40**

Jesus said the goal isn't to just read the Bible—the goal is to find Him. The goal isn't to pray for an hour—the goal is to meet with Him. The goal isn't to just go serve—the goal is to serve with Him. He said we have missed the whole relationship side of things.

Give God Your Whole Heart

When you give God your heart, go all in. Listen, falling in love with God doesn't work unless you go all in. If you go ninety percent in, you're going to say, "Well, that's not very fun and it didn't work so well," because you didn't give Him your all. Consider this verse:

> *"You will seek me and find me when you seek me with all*
> *your heart. I will be found by you," declares the LORD...*
> **—Jeremiah 29:13–14**

If you seek Him with part of your heart, you'll never find Him. You will be one of those who burn out and fade away. God is saying, "I can be found. You and I can have a fantastic relationship if you give your all in your relationship with Me."

Relationship changes everything.

WORKBOOK

Chapter Three Questions

Question: Describe the father you had growing up (or a father figure, if applicable). What misunderstandings about God's character might you carry because of struggles in your relationship with your earthly father? Now describe the best father-child relationship that you have experienced or observed. What does this teach you about being a child of God?

_____

_____

_____

_____

_____

_____

_____

_____

_____

_____

_____

Question: Do you see Christian service as something to be done by paid professionals or as the "family business" of which you are a vital part? What are some gifts, talents, and burdens that God has specifically given you that you can use in working *with* God?

_____

_____

_____

_____

_____

_____

_____

_____

_____

_____

_____

Question: What is the difference between someone who is serving God out of delight, desire, and devotion compared to a person who is serving God out of duty, demand,

and drudgery? In real life situations, how do these differences become apparent? Give examples of when you yourself (or someone you know) have worked for God out of these differing motivations.

_____

_____

_____

_____

_____

_____

_____

_____

_____

_____

_____

_____

Action: Look at Jesus' fifteen references to God as a Father in Matthew 5–7 (the Sermon on the Mount). Write down what each of these verses tells you about the kind of relationship God desires to have with you.

Chapter Three Notes

CHAPTER FOUR

We Is Better than Me

And now these three remain: faith, hope and love. But the greatest of these is love.
—1 Corinthians 13:13

Let love be your greatest aim...
—1 Corinthians 14:1 *(TLB)*

I want you to think about these Scriptures for just a moment. Love is the greatest. Make love the real target. Make love the thing you're trying to accomplish the most. Make love your greatest aim.

What do these verses really mean? What is God trying to say to us? Here's what I think: We as individuals, and certainly as Christians, have made our aim a whole lot of things other than love. If you were to ask someone what being a committed Christian looks like, what answers would you have expected? What would you have said?

You'd probably say that a committed Christian goes to

church all the time. You might say a committed Christian understands the Bible inside and out and has memorized a lot of verses.

But if you search the Scriptures to find out what God's answer is, you'll find that it's far removed from the list above. In fact, what you'll discover from the Bible is that being a Christian is not about what you know as much as it is about how you love.

What you'll discover is that God is less concerned about your knowledge of Scripture and more focused on how you treat people.

Let's look at a few important scriptures from this perspective. I'll tell you upfront, these verses knocked me out. I had to stop about ten times during my study and pause to speak with the Lord and pray. Look at this first one, in the Gospel of Matthew:

> *Therefore, if you are offering your gift at the altar [that's the biblical way of saying you're going to church] and there remember that your brother or sister has something against you, leave your gift there in front of the altar. First go and be reconciled to them; then come [back to church] and offer your gift.*
> **—Matthew 5:23–24**

What was Jesus saying here? He was basically saying, "Don't try to come to talk to Me until you first go settle your issues with people." That's strong language telling us we shouldn't pray and spend time with the Lord until we've settled matters with others. Look at this next one:

Anyone who claims to be in the light but hates a brother or sister is still in the darkness. Anyone who loves their brother and sister lives in the light, and there is nothing in them to make them stumble. But anyone who hates a brother or sister is in the darkness and walks around in the darkness. They do not know where they are going, because the darkness has blinded them.

—1 John 2:9-11

In other words, you're deceived. Darkness has blinded you if you don't have love for others. The Bible says you are virtually blind without love.

In Matthew 22, Jesus was approached by a religious scholar. This academic would be a seminary professor in our day, asking Jesus, "Teacher, You know about all the laws of the Old Testament. Can You give us the CliffsNotes?" Jesus responded:

"Love the Lord your God with all your heart and with all your soul and with all your mind." This is the first and greatest commandment. And the second is like it: "Love your neighbor [other people] as [to the same degree that you care about] yourself."

—Matthew 22:37-39

Jesus says there is a measuring stick for measuring our relationship with God. The determining measurement is that true Christianity, true love, is expressed in the way we treat people. It is not enough to just be nice once in a while, but we are called to actually love our neighbors to the same degree that we love ourselves. As Christians we should desire to go deeper into the things of God, and there is nothing deeper than loving God and loving His people.

Christianity is not about knowledge and a thorough understanding of the Bible. It's about what's happening on the inside of the heart. It's about your love for God and your expression of that love for other people.

The Importance of Love

Let's build a scriptural basis here so we can get practical. We are going to break down what is called the "love chapter," 1 Corinthians 13.

> *If I speak in the tongues of men or of angels, but do not have love, I am only a resounding gong or a clanging cymbal. If I have the gift of prophecy and can fathom all mysteries and all knowledge, and if I have a faith that can move mountains, but do not have love, I am nothing. If I give all I possess to the poor and give over my body to hardship that I may boast, but do not have love, I gain nothing.*
>
> *Love is patient, love is kind. It does not envy, it does not boast, it is not proud. It does not dishonor others, it is not self-seeking, it is not easily angered, it keeps no record of wrongs. Love does not delight in evil but rejoices with the truth. It always protects, always trusts, always hopes, always perseveres.*
>
> *Love never fails. But where there are prophecies, they will cease; where there are tongues, they will be stilled; where there is knowledge, it will pass away. For we know in part and we prophesy in part, but when completeness comes, what is in part disappears. When I was a child, I talked like a child, I thought like a child, I reasoned like a child. When I became a man, I put the ways of childhood behind me. For now we see only a reflection as in a mirror; then we shall see face to face. Now I know in part; then I shall know fully, even as I am fully known.*

*And now these three remain: faith, hope and love. But the
greatest of these is love.*
—1 Corinthians 13:1–13

There are five truths that show the importance of love,
which we can take away from this passage.

1. Without Love, All I Say Is Ineffective

*If I speak in the tongues of men or of angels, but do have
not love, I am only a resounding gong or a clanging cym-
bal.*
—1 Corinthians 13:1

The Bible here is clear. If you're a great communicator,
words aren't the key. It is the heart behind the words that
God is looking at. What we say is not as important as the
motive behind what we say.

That is why the Bible says to speak truth (1 John 3:18;
Ephesians 4:15, 25). But don't stop there. Be a truth person. Sometimes I tell it how it is, no matter how hard the
truth can be. Why? Because I've learned that no matter
how much trouble I get in when I admit my sin, it only
gets worse when I lie.

I also apply this scripture to telling "hard truths." Some
people need to know their life is heading toward a brick
wall, and we would be doing them a disservice by telling
them otherwise. The key to telling hard truths, however,
is Ephesians 4:15, which advises us to speak "the truth in
love." We must approach people with the truth in the spirit
of love.

This is one reason I despise doctrinal debate—because

the angry fights go against this principle. We think the goal is to be right, but that's not the goal according to the Bible. The goal, the aim, is love. Not correctness. *Love.*

2. Without Love, All I Know Is Incomplete

There is an inordinate passion in our society and culture for more knowledge. We have access to information and knowledge more readily than ever before in history. And I think we measure Christianity based on what fits into our brains or how quickly we can find information. We enjoy the feeling of learning more and obtaining more knowledge.

We are knowledge junkies. It feels good to know the right verses and where to apply them, but sometimes we put too much value on information. I love doctrine. But the goal isn't simply to get smarter. The goal isn't to study the Bible more just for the sake of studying. Studying the Bible is an important thing to do, and I'm an advocate for studying the Bible. I'm not discounting personal study, but remember that the ultimate aim is love. First Corinthians says it this way:

> *If I have the gift of prophecy, and can fathom all mysteries and all knowledge ... but do not have love, I am nothing.*
> **—1 Corinthians 13:2**

You could be a Bible scholar and miss the point Paul is making in this passage. The church must be careful. I see Christians struggling with loving our doctrine more than we love God and love people. And I think this was a similar pitfall of the religious people in Jesus' time. We love our particular brand of truth, or our brand of church or of preaching, more than the biggest idea of Scripture—to love God and love others (Matthew 22:36–40).

Too many of us become stale Christians because we are more concerned with knowledge than with love. Knowledge is not the ultimate goal; it is not the big idea of Christianity. The big idea is love. That's why the Bible says that "knowledge puffs up while love builds up" (1 Corinthians 8:1b). Knowing things leads to pride, while love helps others.

3. Without Love, All I Believe Is Insufficient

> ...and if I have a faith that can move mountains, but do not have love, I am nothing.
> —*1 Corinthians 13:2*

Some people erroneously believe that the secret to Christianity is their belief system. All they need to do is simply believe in God. I've got bad news for you on that front: the devil believes in God, too (James 2:19). Just believing in God is not enough.

As I mentioned previously, there is a tangible, measurable attribute that illustrates your relationship with God—how you treat God and how you treat people. Your actions are an extension of your belief system. That's why the Bible says in Galatians 5:6, "The only thing that counts is faith expressing itself through love."

This means that the only thing that counts is love. It's not the fact that you wear the Christian label, attend church, or that you're a believer. The one thing that has a tangible, measurable expression to our world and to God is our faith expressed in love. Hopefully this is motivating you to see how important this topic is.

Without love, all that we know is incomplete. All that we believe is insufficient.

4. Without Love, All I Give Is Insignificant

If I give all I possess to the poor ... but do not have love, I gain nothing.
—1 Corinthians 13:3

Isn't that huge? God still doesn't use giving to the poor or doing good deeds as the measuring stick.

Why be generous? Tax deductions? Why give to the poor? Looking good to others? But what good is a tax deduction to God? What does your pride have to do with glorifying God? That's why He looks at your motives, your love. If you are only generous when others are looking, what good is that? It's insignificant.

But with love, our generosity is sweet to the Lord.

5. Without Love, All I Accomplish Is Inadequate

You may be on a journey of trying to perfect your faith, become more holy and righteous, or even know God more, but you're coming up empty. These are great pursuits, and yet, as we've been discovering, they're not enough. Perhaps you've even tried to chase some things in life that you were sure were going to make you happy, such as success, money, or your career. All those things are wonderful things, yet you're still coming up empty. Perhaps you're starting to realize that there's a void in your heart. Something's missing.

The Bible makes this very clear when it says:

> *[Even if I] give my body to be burned, but have not love, it profits me nothing.*
> **—1 Corinthians 13:3** *(NKJV)*

Do you know what that means? Love is life's greatest aim. For some of us, the devil has come into our lives through a series of sad circumstances, people, or events, and our hearts are a mess. We may know the Bible more than we have ever known it before, but we know something's still missing. Love.

My prayer for you is that your capacity to be loved, and to love, would grow. Maybe there's something inside you that's been walled up or hurt or messed up, and your life's metaphorical bank account is overdrawn. You may be getting some other things in your life right, but for some reason, life in general is not working and you've come to the conclusion that there's a zero on your personal balance sheet.

God is going to audit each one of us one day. The Bible calls it Judgment Day, at which time I believe we'll be given two questions to answer.[13]

The first question: "Did you believe in My Son? Did you have a relationship with Him?" Your answer will determine where you will spend eternity and whether or not you get asked the second question (Matthew 7:21–23).

If your response indicates that you did not believe in Jesus, you're not going to be saved and get to experience life in heaven; rather, you'll be sent to eternal punishment.

But those who respond that they believe in Jesus and invited Him into their lives will get to enter heaven and live eternally with Him. But they will have to respond to the second question: "What did you do with your life?" The Bible calls this the judgment seat of Christ, and it's a judgment for Christians (2 Corinthians 5:10) and an audit of our earthly life.

We will be measured by how we loved and how we treated people (Matthew 25:31–46). When it's my time to answer to God, I want to be able to tell him I spent my life earnestly trying to reflect His love to His children—my neighbors.

The Bible is clear on the value God places on love:

Love knows no limit to its endurance, no end to its trust, no fading of its hope; it can outlast anything. It is, in fact, the one thing that still stands when all else has fallen.
—1 Corinthians 13:7–8a (PHILLIPS)

I want to encourage you to not be the type of Christian who just shows up at church. Be the type of Christian who is focused on love every day and everywhere: when you're stuck in traffic, when you're with that person who's a thorn in your side, when you've been wronged, when you're angry, when you're grumpy on a Monday morning—and the list goes on and on. Love is my passion in life because without love, the gospel message means nothing. Honestly, church means nothing to me if this message doesn't work on Monday morning in my life.

You see, real love is not what the world makes it out to be. It's not roses and candles and chocolates, and it's not me loving tacos or even loving my wife. Love is not a feeling; it's much greater than a mere emotion. In fact, the word *love* in this scripture is the Greek word *agape*, which indicates unconditional love. In Scripture, we see this best in Romans 5:8: "But God demonstrates His own love toward us, in that while we were still sinners, Christ died for us" (NKJV).

Agape Is Unconditional Love

Agape means that we aren't going to wait for the feeling before we act in love. But we often do just the opposite and wait for the emotion to overcome us so we can then react. We react to the feeling in our heart, but that's not true love. In fact, true love is behaving in love even when you don't feel it. Real love is when you get up in the middle of the night with a sick child. Love is cleaning up the mess of a sick church member. Love is visiting older folks in the nursing home. Love is being nice to your neighbors in the morning when they've kept you up all night. Love says, "I care about you, and I will do this for you," even when you don't feel like doing it.

The word *agape* is used in John 15, where Jesus says that "Greater [agape; unconditional] love has no one than this: to lay down one's life for one's friends" (John 15:13).

That's exactly what Jesus did. It amazes me how many people still don't even respond to the love of God. I personally believe it's because of religion. Religion is the biggest culprit because many churches send the message of: "You get it right first and I'll accept you," and it's just not what God says. The Bible says that Jesus went to the cross for us while we were still sinning (Romans 5:8).

Jesus didn't ask for a show of hands to determine if His sacrifice would be received. Mankind was still sinning in the midst of Him being spit on, beaten, and tortured. He went to the cross to pay for the guy who was hitting Him in the face.

Jesus' sacrifice is the greatest ever expression of love. You may be thinking, "Yeah, but that's Jesus. He's God. Only He can love that way." Jesus said in John 13:

A new commandment I give you: Love one another [unconditionally]. As I have [unconditionally] loved you, so you must [unconditionally] love one another.
—John 13:34

Love is tangible. It's incredibly measurable. That's why the love chapter says these words:

Love is patient, love is kind. It does not envy, it does not boast, it is not proud. It does not dishonor others, it is not self-seeking, it is not easily angered, it keeps no record of wrongs. Love does not delight in evil but rejoices with the truth. It always protects, always trusts, always hopes, always perseveres.

Love never fails.

—1 Corinthians 13:4–8a

Practical Application

True love can be defined in two ways.

1. Love Is an Action

You see, love is not something you say, know, believe, or accomplish. It's doing something. You're going to get an opportunity today to do something for someone, a random act of kindness. Sit with a neighbor who has cancer or clean a sick person's bathroom. Perhaps it's watching a couple's kids while they go to counseling. Or maybe it's to say nothing when you have the right to be angry.

First John says it this way: "Dear children, let us not love with [just] words or speech but with actions and in truth" (1 John 3:18).

Love is an action. Just look at that action list from 1 Corinthians 13. Start there. I'm most convicted about the statements telling us that love is supposed to be patient and not easily angered. Pick a few for yourself on that list and realize it's an action.

Love doesn't wait for a feeling. Love doesn't say, "First, let me wait for the emotion inside of me, then I'll treat you the way I should."

2. Love Is a Choice

Love is not an emotion! We state, "I fell in love,"

which sounds like love is a hole that we fell into. You don't fall in love! That's not how it works with true *agape* love. Love is a choice. Wouldn't you agree with me that love is purer when you don't feel like doing it? Honestly, love is probably as far away from feelings as you can possibly get. "And over all these virtues put on love, which binds them all together in perfect unity" (Colossians 3:14).

As God's children, let's consider our lives on earth a journey, with love as the goal—the target of our existence.

WORKBOOK

Chapter Four Questions

Question: Do you have relationships that are burdened by unresolved issues? Are you trying to worship and serve God, but refusing to make things right with another believer? Why, and in what ways, does conflict with another person disrupt your relationship with God?

_____

_____

_____

_____

_____

_____

_____

_____

_____

_____

_____

Question: Describe a time when someone communicated truth to you but in a manner devoid of love. What was your response? How might the same message have been delivered in a loving way, and how could the right attitude have made a difference?

_____

_____

_____

_____

_____

_____

_____

_____

_____

_____

_____

Question: What are some things you use to measure your Christianity, such as reading devotionals or the Bible, attending a class or completing a course, making sacrifices of finances and/or time, or serving in or establishing a particular program or ministry initiative? Is the goal and purpose of each of these things greater love for God and others? Are they reaching, or falling short of, the ultimate goal? How can you make *love* your motivation and the measuring stick for everything you do?

_____

_____

_____

_____

_____

_____

_____

_____

_____

_____

_____

Action: Love is an action and a choice, not a feeling. Make a list of three love choices you will make this week—one for a family member, one for a church friend, and one for an unbeliever. As you take on each action, ask God to make you a reflection of His love and to keep your heart free from selfishness.

Chapter Four Notes

CHAPTER FIVE

Don't Walk Alone

Making a decision about a relationship is a big deal. In fact, it's downright scary. Now, if we are honest, we have all experienced pain, brokenness, or even the death of someone we love. And no doubt all of us have exchanged harsh words we are ashamed of. In spite of our best intentions, nobody escapes difficulties in a relationship.

Many people shy away from being hurt again and conclude: "The most important relationship I have is with myself. I'm going to take care of me."

So, they make their marriage and kids disposable. "If you cross the line, family member, I'll push you out of my life." Or, "Boss, I'm loyal, but don't push me too far." And we develop this attitude of, "I'm just going to watch out for me."

In today's culture we are surrounded by people, yet we are alone. We live in populated cities, but we brush right by others. We sit in crowded cafés, and we look at social media on our phones or laptops. Houses are built within feet of each other, and we never talk to our neighbors.

You may spend your days sitting next to people, and you might have people in your life, but there's a good chance you've gotten to a place where you're alone. Most of the time, we distance ourselves as a way of protection. Unfortunately, it doesn't help. In fact, it's hurts.

Relationship Excuses

I want to show you a verse that's incredibly powerful from the book of Ecclesiastes, written by the wisest person who ever lived, Solomon. He was a king in Israel, the son of David. God told Solomon He would grant one request, and Solomon asked for wisdom. God granted his wish, and Solomon became known for his wisdom throughout the world, both then and today (1 Kings 3:1–15). Solomon said:

> *There was a man all alone; he had neither son nor brother. There was no end to his toil, yet his eyes were not content with his wealth.*
> *—Ecclesiastes 4:8a*

In other words, life simply did not work out, so he tried to force life to succeed by focusing on things other than relationships. He found out though that even his eyes were unsatisfied with wealth; although he tried to go after satisfaction in other areas outside of relationships, he was not fulfilled. It's the same with us. We were designed to be in relationships. And because we were designed to be in relationships, choosing to love unconditionally is one of the most important decisions of our lives. Relationships are good and should be a priority. But a lot of us make excuses, like these:

I Don't Need People

You may feel that going to church on Sunday is enough to fill your relationship tank. Perhaps you think you don't need people beyond any interactions you have at a Sunday service.

A big church is good, but it's easy to get lost. We need small groups. We need small church. Small church is the term I like to use for small groups within a church body—it's where people break into tiny groups and study the Word, share prayer requests, and spend time together outside of the Sunday service. You can be a member of a big church and still make room for small church. Why is this important? Because we all have four areas of our lives:

*1. We all have what I call the **arena** of our lives.* The arena area of your life is the part of you that is readily available for everyone. It is the "I know and you know" aspect of yourself. When you attend a big church, you never go beyond the arena with others—you simply smile and don't get to know people deeply.

*2. We all wear **masks**.* Masks are the parts of yourself you keep hidden unless you are with trusted people. Your masks are the "I know and you don't know" part of yourself. When you participate in small church, it's a place to take off your mask and be real.

*3. The third area of our lives is **blind spots**.* These are the aspects of yourself that you are ignorant of, but others have insight into. They are the, "I don't know but you know" parts of your life. Being a part of small church allows you to grow close enough to others so they can see things in your life you may not be able to spot. It also develops the trust necessary to openly communicate about those areas of your life.

*4. And finally, we all have **potential**.* Potential is the unknown in life; it's the "I don't know and you don't know" part of existence. Connecting with others in small church may open up lifelong friendships and doors of opportunity that you may not expect.

You must be in an environment where these four areas of your life can be discovered and developed, and three out of the four can only happen in a small church or small group setting.

As iron sharpens iron, so one person sharpens another.
—Proverbs 27:17

I particularly like the story about Muhammed Ali traveling on an airplane when the seat belt light came on. He didn't buckle up, so the flight attendant said, "Sir, you're going to have to buckle up." He responded, "Superman don't need no seat belt." But the flight attendant quickly replied, "And Superman don't need no plane neither, so buckle up!"[14]

Despite your strengths and skills, you're not Superman

(or Superwoman). You need people. We all do. And in a church setting, relationships happen in small church.

I'm Not a People Person

A lot of people use their personality as an excuse to avoid close relationships. You may find yourself saying, "Jason, you're outgoing, you like people. But I'm kind of shy and bashful."

Regardless of your disposition, you need relationships. Is it tough? Yes, forging new and lasting relationships can be awkward for all of us. But it's best for you if you have solid relationships. Never let your personality be an excuse to remain alone in this life. Sometimes we need to stretch ourselves and do hard things. For some people, being friends takes practice. But to say you're not a people person is an excuse to ignore the fact that God commands us to love one another. He will help you connect with the right people.

What's Going to Happen?

Perhaps it is the fear of the unknown that is keeping you from developing deeper relationships with others. Maybe you think, "I've never been to a small group before." "I'm afraid the people there will be a little weird." "I'm afraid I'm going to show up and find a circle of chairs in the living room, and my chair will be the one smack dab in the middle—and everyone will stare at me and expect me to confess my sins!"

That's not what goes on. In fact, the very opposite is

what you're going to discover.

Sometimes there's an activity, like bowling or dinner—doing things people do, but doing it with other Christians. At other times, it's like a book club setting, where you get to talk about what you've read. Some people bring a Bible. Others just talk about work. Usually, someone brings a devotional.

It's an open atmosphere with no judgment. You'll discover that whenever you do share, you're not going to get condemnation in return. Instead, you'll get people who love you and say, "I've been there. I've done that. I've experienced that, too." This C.S. Lewis quote is one of my favorites: "The typical expression of opening friendship would be something like, 'What! You too? I thought I was the only one.'"[15]

Such non-judgmental friendships are what you'll discover. No one is perfect, not me and not you. All of God's children have issues. We all need a place where we can say, "I'm really mad" and have people listen without condemning us. Let people into your life, and encourage others by joining a small group.

It Didn't Work Last Time

Maybe you got burned in the past and you are scared to reach out and develop new friendships. Satan wins if you isolate yourself. The devil uses any pain you've experienced due to a broken relationship for more devious outcomes than just hurting that relationship alone. Satan is trying to keep you from ever being in a relationship again.

If a church hurts you—really, it's the people in the church—Satan has a plan. He is looking down the line. He wants to make sure that you hurt so badly you never connect to the things of God ever again and miss the best of what God wants to give you. He causes divides and hard feelings through relationships. Why? Because relationships are powerful and important, so he *must* attack them. Nothing can stop a good relationship.

But we let petty issues become issues that control our lives. Instead, we need to look past those issues and let God heal us. We need to deal with the pain and then move beyond it, so we can receive God's blessings. Don't let past wounds and experiences stop you from reaching your potential.

I Don't Have the Time

Perhaps you feel like you can't fit another person into your life. Maybe you're thinking, "I'm raising three kids, and I've got a lot going on. I'm not looking for another relationship right now." But there are some relationships you need to make time for, because they will enhance your life.

The Bible talks a lot about our use of time. Be wise in how you act and make the most of your time (Ephesians 5:16). The Psalmist said, "Teach us to number our days and recognize how few they are; help us to spend them as we should" (Psalm 90:12 TLB).

The truth is, if you fit anything into your life, it should be pursuing healthy, God-centered relationships. These relationships are vital. When you get your relationships right, the way God designed them, you'll have loving people to encourage you and watch your back—which is important, because "your enemy the devil prowls around like a roaring lion looking for someone to devour" (1 Peter 5:8). Developing the right relationships is worth the investment!

Relationship Decisions

Offer hospitality to one another without grumbling. Each of you should use whatever gift you have received to serve others, as faithful stewards of God's grace in its various forms. If anyone speaks, they should do so as one who speaks the very words of God. If anyone serves, they should do so with the strength God provides, so that in all things God may be praised through Jesus Christ. To him be the glory and the power for ever and ever. Amen.

—1 Peter 4:9–11

So, when it comes to developing God-centered relationships, where do we begin? Start with these four key types of relationship decision, which I'm convinced everyone has to make at some point in life.

1. Choose to Nurture Important Relationships

I've got a few relationships that are vital. God has made me a dad, a husband, and a pastor. I'm mindful that I can't leave these critical relationships as is. They require attention. If you leave relationships alone, they don't stay the same—they deteriorate. For example, you wouldn't say, "Alright! I wined and dined her, took her out, gave her roses and chocolate, and married her—now nothing more is needed."

Every great relationship happens on purpose, not by accident. The Bible uses the analogy of your body to talk about relationships. It says when you are in a relationship, it's as if you are connected to different parts of the body. Colossians 2:19 says that the whole body is supported and held together by its ligaments and sinews, and it grows as God causes it to grow. You are one of those parts!

We care for our actual bodies with exercise, nutrition, taking care of ourselves, and getting enough sleep. If we care for our bodies properly, we increase our chances of getting to use them for a long time, Lord willing.

Strengthen your relationships like you would your body—nurture them before they break down. Fix your marriage before it needs fixing. Don't show up in the counseling office with pieces all over the place, and say, "Here, put this back together." You must do the upkeep. Don't wait for the car engine to fall on the street, change the oil. Practice preventive maintenance. Nurture your relationships. Relationships need a fresh log on the fire now and again to burn brightly. You don't wait till it burns out to add a log—you add it while it's still burning.

If you are a parent, don't wait until your children have issues before working on your relationship with them. Grow close to your kids now. Spend time with them and nurture them. As a parent, I have three things that are my aim. First, that they would love God passionately and have a personal relationship with Him where they read the Word, pray, fast, and want to spend time with Him. Secondly, that they love me and their mom. And third, that they would love the church. If I can do those three things, I will have succeeded as a parent, but it takes time.

The same is true with other relationships as well. From parent to children, to husband and wife, pastor and congregations, to best friends, every relationship needs to be stoked before problems arise. So nurture your important relationships.

2. Choose to Restore Your Broken Relationships

Most people have broken relationships that need to be restored. Some of you are already feeling the pain of hard times in a relationship right now. Let me say something very clearly to you—the pains of an unresolved conflict are greater than the short pain and final relief of a resolved conflict. The pain you're currently experiencing is greater than the pain of fixing the problem.

I'm going to urge you to do your part. If the other person doesn't cooperate—and many times, they don't—you still need to make a decision that you won't hold onto the pain and record of wrongdoings. Instead, practice Romans 12:

Do not repay anyone evil for evil. ... If it is possible, as far as it depends on you, live at peace with everyone.
—Romans 12:17a–18

Decide that you're going to be that person who just doesn't hold onto things. Forgiveness is a choice. Resolving conflict is not an event; it's a choice. And you need to make that choice.

One of my favorite stories is of a couple celebrating their fiftieth wedding anniversary. At the celebration someone asked the woman what the secret was to sticking it out with her husband for fifty years. She said, "Oh, that's easy. When we first got married, I decided that I would make a list of his ten greatest faults and that I would overlook those ten things for the rest of our lives. For the sake of our marriage, I did."

Someone asked, "Well, what were the ten things?" She replied, "You know, I never made the list. Every time he did something, I just thought, 'Well, lucky for him, that's on the list.'"

Why not live that way? "Lucky for you, that's just one of those things I don't hang on to and that I'm going to let God handle." You will be so happy when you start to live this way! Give it a try and see for yourself.

3. Choose to Sever Harmful Relationships

Some of you are in harmful relationships that are not good for you. If you hang around those people much longer, you're going to go down with them. You know what I'm talking about. That flirtatious relationship at the job when you're already married. That guy who always tells those sleazy jokes. The person who makes hateful comments. At some point, you need to decide, "I'm not having junk in my life." It may be hard, but ridding yourself of the relationships that cause you harm will benefit you.

The Bible has so much to say about good relationships

and their benefits.

> *A mirror reflects a man's face, but what he is really like is shown by the kind of friends he chooses.*
> **—Proverbs 27:19** (TLB)

Show me your friends, and I'll show you your future. That's a fact.

> *Walk with the wise and become wise, for a companion of fools suffers harm.*
> **—Proverbs 13:20**

> *Do not be yoked together with unbelievers. For what do righteousness and wickedness have in common? Or what fellowship can light have with darkness?*
> **—2 Corinthians 6:14**

Wickedness and righteousness can't exist together. So, what do you do when you're being abused? When you're emotionally downtrodden? When someone is simply using you? You get rid of the godless relationship. You sever it! You say, "I'm not going to have that in my life." You may need to make some hard friend decisions, but get away from harmful relationships unless you want your future to look like that. Decide to sever them.

4. Choose to Initiate Meaningful Relationships

If you don't already have meaningful relationships,

you need them. Hebrews 10 says:

> *And let us consider how we may spur one another on toward love and good deeds, not giving up meeting together, as some are in the habit of doing, but encouraging one another—and all the more as you see the Day approaching.*
> **—Hebrews 10:24–25**

Growing new friendships can be one of the most rewarding activities God has ever commanded. It takes love, dedication, and openness. Don't be afraid! Be friendly to make friends.

Practical Application

Be sure to have your relationships right, because Judgment Day is coming—that's what Hebrews 10:25 is saying in the previous section. There are certain relationships that are crucial. If these meaningful relationships do not exist in your life, begin taking steps now to make sure they happen this year.

Build a Relationship with a Church

You shouldn't merely go to church. You need a relationship with a church. There's a big difference. So, if you're church hopping, stop. Find one and get in it. Get into a small group, and find your spiritual gifts and purpose. Get involved: serve on ministry teams, go to church events. Just do it! I promise you, at the end of a year, maybe you're not where you want to be, but you'll look back and recognize that your life is richer.

Build a Relationship with a Small Group

A relationship with a small group can change your life. The right group will provide you with encouragement. They will have your back and give you strength, prayer, and support. Who doesn't want all that?

UCLA recently did a study that said you need eight to ten meaningful touches every day, just to be healthy. You need affection eight to ten times a day![16] We're made to be social creatures, and even if we're not in an environment that enjoys handshakes or hugs, we still need to be heard and to listen. Small groups do just that.

You need encouragement in your life. Pick a group, give it a couple of weeks, and I'm telling you, you'll make some of the best friends you've ever had in your life.

Build a Relationship with a Team

Everybody needs to be on a team. You know why? Teams are fun! And teams allow us to produce more with our life than we will ever be able to produce alone. By yourself, you will have limited production. But if you get on a team—a technical team, a parking team, a children's team, a worship team, a small group team—you will accomplish so much more. You'll love doing something that is making a difference and is productive!

Build Your Relationship with God

You don't need a religion. You need to be in a relationship with God. You ought to be blown away by the fact that He wants to be in a relationship with you. He loves you and wants to bless you. He wants to know you. He wants to talk to you. He wants you to talk to Him.

If there's a single message that I want you to hear, it's that relationship is miles apart from religion. It's intimate, it's fun, it's meaningful, and it's real. Reflect and determine if you have a personal relationship with Jesus or if you are just participating in religion. You could just be attending church and going through the motions, and, if so, you're missing the joy of knowing God. If that's the case, make the decision to accept His unconditional love and pursue Him. All you need to do is love Him back.

Chapter Five Questions

Question: Describe a relationship that ended painfully for you. What walls did you set up to protect yourself from future hurt or disappointment? How have those walls impacted your current relationships and potential future relationships?

_____

_____

_____

_____

_____

_____

_____

_____

_____

_____

Question: Which excuses listed in this chapter are you most inclined toward?

- I don't need people
- I'm not a people person
- What's going to happen?
- It didn't work last time
- I don't have time

How can you replace that wrong thinking with truthful thinking about the importance of relationships for your life?

_____

_____

_____

_____

_____

_____

_____

_____

_____

_____

_____

Question: When is it time to sever a damaging relation-ship? How can you show Christ to the harmful person without being harmed yourself? What are some scriptural and common-sense boundaries when dealing with these types of relationships? Check out the book of Proverbs for wise guidance on the type of people to avoid.

_____

_____

_____

_____

_____

_____

_____

_____

_____

_____

_____

Action: List the five to seven most important relation-ships in your life (immediate family, extended family, friends, or someone you are mentoring. If you can't think of that many, you might need to make the decision to initiate some more meaningful relationships!). What are you doing to intentionally nurture each of these relationships? Write down an intentional step you will take this week. How can you make nurturing your relationships a regular part of your life instead of hoping it will happen by accident?

Chapter Five Notes

CHAPTER SIX

Change the World

Can you imagine being a U.S. ambassador? As an ambassador, you're never truly off duty. You are always representing your country everywhere you go. You can't be cranky to your barista in the morning or rude to your waitress at the restaurant. Everything you do is a reflection of your country and you might be the only representative others ever encounter.

The Bible says in 2 Corinthians 5:20, "We are therefore Christ's ambassadors." What is an ambassador? An ambassador is a representative sent out on a mission to build relationships.

There are political ambassadors. There are economic and business ambassadors. There are cultural and goodwill ambassadors. And the Bible says there are spiritual ambassadors. We are Christ's ambassadors. If you are a follower of Christ, the Bible says you are an ambassador for Him in the world.

An Ambassador for Christ

I want to study four aspects of being a Christian, of being an ambassador for Christ. Within these four aspects, we will determine the role, the responsibilities, and the rewards of being an ambassador of Jesus Christ.

1. As an Ambassador, You Are a Representative of Jesus

To understand your role as representative, you need to understand the difference between your career and your calling. You might work as an insurance salesman, but you're not called to be an insurance salesman. There's a difference between your work for wages and your calling to serve God.

Years ago, when I worked for a respiratory company, I was talking to my employees and I admitted to them, "I'm an ambassador for Jesus, disguised as a manager."

So what's your disguise? There's no changing the fact that you are an ambassador for Jesus. If you're a follower of Christ, that's your primary calling. But you may be disguised as a mom, nurse, truck driver, mechanic, realtor, salesman, or whatever. That's your job, your career. No matter how much you enjoy your job, that's not your calling.

I looked up the word *calling* and what the Bible says about what we're called to do. The Bible says this in several passages:

- We are called to be His holy people (Romans

1:7).

- We are called to be God's friends (John 15:14–15).

- We are called to be holy (1 Corinthians 1:2).

- We are called into fellowship with Jesus (1 Corinthians 1:9).

- We are called to speak for Christ (2 Corinthians 5:19–20).

- We are called to serve each other (Galatians 5:13).

- We are called to live in peace (Romans 12:18; Colossians 3:15).

- We are called to become like Jesus for God's purpose (Romans 8:28).

- We are called to suffer for Him (1 Peter 2:21).

- We are called to bless those who curse us (Romans 4:7; 1 Peter 3:9).

- We are called to eternal life (1 Timothy 1:16).

- We are called to share His glory (2 Thessalonians 2:14).

If you are a follower of Jesus Christ, you are a representative of Jesus Christ. You are an ambassador. You have an assignment, which is to build relationships that will draw others to Christ.

If you're going to follow Jesus as an ambassador, it

should affect the way you live and perhaps radically change your life. In fact, the Bible says this in Philippians 1:27: "Be sure that you live in a way that brings honor to the Good News of Christ" (ICB). If you're going to be an ambassador, a representative of Jesus, you've got to live like it. You can't just name His name without playing the game. You've got to back it up with your life. We need to remember that we represent Jesus.

Each morning before you head off to work or get ready for your day's tasks, tell yourself, " Remember who you represent." When you're out playing a pickup game of ball, remember who you represent. When you go into a grocery store or a movie theater or you're in traffic, re-member who you represent. When you're frustrated with a clerk and you want to let out your frustration, remember who you represent.

The Bible says in Ephesians 4:1 to "live a life worthy of the calling you have received." I have been called to represent Jesus to the world. And so have you. This is not just for pastors. It's for every believer. An ambassador not only represents someone, but also has a job to do.

2. As an Ambassador, You've Been Given a Mission

Ambassadors are sent on diplomatic missions. In fact, the embassies where ambassadors work are called perma-nent missions—the permanent mission to China, the permanent mission to Australia, the permanent mission to Israel, the permanent mission to wherever. The word *mission* is what an ambassador does.

Jesus said in John 17:18–19, "In the same way that you

gave me a mission in the world, I give them a mission in the world" (MSG). Did you know that you have a mission? The moment you step across the line spiritually and you become a follower of Jesus, God has a mission for your life. Your mission is to be His ambassador.

When you're on a mission, the mission is all that matters. You're not there to simply view the scenery. You're not there to take pictures. You're not there to sample the local cuisine. As an ambassador, you're there on a mission. When soldiers are deployed overseas, they aren't sent there just to see the world. They're sent by their country to get a job done. They're not there just sitting around drinking martinis or margaritas and listening to Jimmy Buffett. They're actually working. They have a mission to accomplish.

Of all of the missions in the world, the most important mission of all is helping people get to know God and settle their eternal destinies. We are only going to be on earth for about sixty or eighty years, but we are going to be in eternity forever. So, our mission as ambassadors of Christ is the most important. Eternity makes a mission to the moon or a mission to some other country seem small and insignificant.

Paul wrote, "I don't care about my own life. The most important thing is that I complete my mission, the work that the Lord Jesus gave me—to tell other people the Good News about God's grace" (Acts 20:24 ICB). He said that his job was to complete his mission. At the end of his life, Paul said, "I have finished the race..." (2 Timothy 4:7). He completed his mission. He knew he had done what God told him to do.

Are you going to be able to say the same? One day when you stand before God, He's going to ask, "Did you complete the mission I gave you?" Some will say, "Oh! I didn't even know I had a mission." But God did not put us on earth just to live for ourselves. The Bible says we are not only responsible with the mission of representing Jesus, but also with the message as well.

3. As an Ambassador, You've Been Given Authority to Speak

Sometimes we don't feel very confident talking about God to other people. Maybe we feel a little insecure or unsure or timid and hesitant. You may think, "Who am I to talk to somebody about Jesus? I don't know what to say or how to say it." And so we say nothing.

But God says that he authorizes us and empowers us to speak for Him.

In Matthew 28 Jesus powerfully inspires us this way:

> *All authority in heaven and on earth has been given to me. Therefore go and make disciples of all nations, baptizing them in the name of the Father and of the Son and of the Holy Spirit, and teaching them to obey everything I have commanded you. And surely I am with you always, to the very end of the age.*
> **—Matthew 28:18b–20**

That verse is called the Great Commission. It is our co-mission. It is our mission in life. The Great Commission was not given to pastors. It was not given to missionaries.

It was not given to priests or elders or professional evangelists. Jesus gave the Great Commission to every one of His followers. It's your commission. One day God's going to ask, "Did you do the commission I gave you? Did you do the mission I had for you? Somebody gave you the good news because they represented Me. Did you pass it on? Did you share it with anybody else?"

The Bible teaches this over and over. God authorizes you to speak on His behalf. You don't have to go check with anybody else. You can talk in the name of Christ to other people. He says you represent Him. He has given you a mission and He has given you the authority to speak.

4. As an Ambassador, You Serve in a Foreign Culture

If you are a believer, a follower of Jesus Christ, your home is not on earth. Your home is in heaven. Your homeland is in heaven, and your identity is in eternity (Hebrews 13:14; Philippians 3:20).

Do ambassadors live in their home countries or in foreign countries? They live in foreign countries. So, for instance, America's ambassador to China lives in China. In fact, they often live in enemy territory. During the Cold War, American ambassadors lived in all the communist nations, even though they were our enemies and were actually trying to bring the United States down. Men like Foy D. Kohler were in the Soviet Union while the Cuban Missile Crisis brought the two superpowers to the brink of nuclear war. So, like Kohler, an ambassador will often live not just in a foreign country or culture, but in an alien or enemy culture during crisis times.

The Bible says in 1 Peter 1:17, "So if you call God your Father, live your time as temporary residents on earth..." (GW). An ambassador doesn't buy a permanent home. You're on a short-term assignment in a foreign culture, and you're not in your homeland setting down roots.

Jesus is telling us not to get too comfortable living in this world. You're just an ambassador. Don't think that this life on earth is all there is. Don't get sucked into the myth that the here and now is everything. Don't forget your role. Your role is not to create a little cushy pad and make your life as comfortable as possible. God says your role as an ambassador is to represent Him, to fulfill His mission, and to speak in His name with authority. And remember that you're doing it in foreign territory.

Philippians 3:17–21 contrasts the mindset of believers and unbelievers: unbelievers consider life as existing only here on earth, while believers think of themselves as citizens of heaven, where the Lord Jesus Christ lives.

What are you supposed to do while you are here? After you become a believer, after you accept God's salvation, once your sins are forgiven and you know you're going to heaven, why doesn't God just take you right then? Ultimately you're going to heaven anyway, so why should He leave you here for another twenty, thirty, forty, or however many years with all the sin, suffering, sorrow, sadness, depression, despair, discouragement, problems, pressures, difficulties, trials, tribulations, and tears? Once you're in, why does He leave you here on earth?

To be an ambassador.

Heaven is perfect. You can have fun in heaven. You can sleep, rest, and fellowship with other people in heaven. You can pray, you can worship, and you can be creative in heaven. There is eating in heaven—with no calories. There are only two things you cannot do in heaven. One of them is sin, because it's a perfect place. And the other is be an ambassador to unbelievers—to tell people the good news who don't already know it. Which of those two do you think God leaves you here to do?

Practical Application

As an ambassador, you have three responsibilities here on earth.

1. You Must Be an Example

You must set an example for other people. The first thing God wants you to do is to help other people know what He is like by showing His character in your life— love, joy, peace, patience, gentleness, goodness, faithfulness, kindness, meekness, self-control (Galatians 5:22–23).

The Bible says in 1 Peter 2:11–12 that there are unbelievers living all around you who might say you're doing wrong by following Christ. So, live such good lives that they'll see the good things you do and will give glory to God.

What does that mean? The first job of an ambassador, whether it's to a country or for Jesus, is to set a good example.

Remember the story at the beginning of the chapter about being an ambassador? As an ambassador, you should understand you're always on duty—always representing your country.

What would happen if you lived your life like an ambassador? What if you realized that you're always on task as an ambassador of Jesus Christ? Would it affect your words and actions if you recognized that you may be the only Christian some people will ever know? To some people around you, you may be the only glimpse of the Bible that they'll ever read. You are a living, breathing, acting Bible. You either make God look good or you make God look bad.

And there are plenty of times when Christians, me included, make God look bad. We say stupid things and we're dogmatic and mean and cranky. That's not good. There's an old proverb that there are two reasons why people don't know the Lord: one of them is they've never met a Christian, and the other is that they have. If someone says "no thanks" to becoming a follower of Jesus because of an interaction with you, then you're not acting as an ambassador of God. Realize your life is to be an example in everything you do.

So my question is, how well does your daily life represent Jesus? Can anybody tell from your example what God is like? When people look at you, can they say, "Jesus must be very kind because you are kind." "Jesus must be very patient because Jesus is in your life and you are patient." "Jesus must be very forgiving because you forgave me when I didn't deserve it." "Jesus must be good because you display goodness in the midst of evil."

In the daily frustrations of life, remember that these are opportunities to display Jesus to the world. When a friend gossips about you, someone accidently rams the back of your car, someone at work makes you look bad, or your spouse says something silly or inconsiderate, keep in mind that you are Christ's ambassador.

What does your life say about God to the people around you? You may not like it, but if you claim to be a follower of Christ, you are an ambassador. You may be a lousy one or you may be a good one, but you are an ambassador. You represent Jesus in everything you do, whether you like it or not.

2. You Must Share the Message

I have a message that God has given me, and He wants me to share it with other people.

It's interesting that in politics or in diplomacy, ambassadors are often used in history to end wars, rather than generals or presidents. Ambassadors are sent to negotiate at the conference table. Ambassadors are sent to sign the peace treaty. Ambassadors are sent to bring reconciliation between warring entities and conflicting groups.

It's not an accident that God chose that term to refer to us as well. We're to help people make peace with God. We're to help people reconcile their relationship with God.

God's very clear about the message he expects you to share:

Therefore, if anyone is in Christ, the new creation has come: The old has gone, the new is here! All this is from God, who reconciled us to himself through Christ and gave

> *us the ministry of reconciliation: that God was reconciling*
> *the world to himself in Christ, not counting the people's*
> *sins against them. And he has committed to us the message*
> *of reconciliation.*
> **—2 Corinthians 5:17–19**

To paraphrase, anyone who has joined Christ becomes a new person. The old person is gone. All this is done by God, who, through Christ, changed the enmity between us into friendship and gave us the task of making others His friends also. We are to spread the message that God wants to make all human beings His friends through Christ. To continue with this passage that is filled with spiritual truths, I'll point out a couple more things.

The first part of the message in this scripture is that Jesus offers everybody a new life. Anybody joined to Christ becomes a new person. This is a message of regeneration, a message of a new birth, the beauty that you get a brand-new life.

Who wouldn't want a chance to start over? Have you ever started either a personal or professional project and realized halfway through that you are unhappy with your progress and want to start over? Or perhaps you're halfway through life and wish you could get a do-over? God says you can. He can give you a brand-new life. Jesus offers a new life to everybody.

The second part of the message in the scripture above is that Jesus ends our war with God. Did you know that you're at war with God until you make peace with Him? Where is the war?

The war is the conflict in your soul over who's going to be God—you or God? The Bible says every human being in all of humanity has fallen short of God's glory (Romans 3:23). Humanity has followed in the footsteps of Satan who said, "I will ascend to the heavens; I will raise my throne above the stars of God... I will ascend above the tops of the clouds; I will make myself like the Most High" (Isaiah 14:13a–14). We don't want God running our lives; we want to run our own lives. We want to make our decisions and don't want God telling us what to do. We want to do what we want to do. That's an attitude that got Satan kicked out of heaven. It's pride. The middle letter of pride is "I" and the middle letter of sin is "I". Basically, *I* cause my problem. And that rebellion against God puts me in a war against God.

You may not realize it, but you're at war with God until you accept what Christ has done for you. The conflict causes self-inflicted problems in your life—unknown stress, the subconscious pressure, the guilt, the fear, the anxiety, all of those different things come from being out of whack with your Creator.

So, we're at war with God, but God wants us as His friends. That's the message of reconciliation. All of our war crimes have been forgiven. God just wipes them out. That's salvation.

How does God do this? He does it through Jesus. And He does it out of love. God was in Christ on earth, making peace between the world and himself through Jesus' sacrifice on the cross. In Christ, God doesn't hold the world guilty of its sins. And He gave us this message of peace:

We are therefore Christ's ambassadors, as though God were making his appeal through us. We implore you on

Christ's behalf: Be reconciled to God. God made him who had no sin to be sin for us, so that in him we might become the righteousness of God.
—2 Corinthians 5:20–21

In other words, we have been sent to speak for Christ. It is as if God is calling to others through us. We speak for Christ when we beg you to be at peace with God. Christ had no sin, but God made Him to become sin so that in Christ, we can become right with God. And now we are workers together with God.

The second thing we are called to do as ambassadors is to share the message. You don't have to go check with anybody else. You are the official ambassador. God has authorized every one of His children to speak on His behalf. You have been given the authority.

3. You Must Show Love

You must show love to everybody. As an ambassador, you've got to have a big heart. Why must an ambassador of Jesus Christ show love to everybody? Because God is love (1 John 4:8). And if you show anything but love to other people, you're not representing Jesus. God is love.

How do I show love to the people in my life—the people I work with, my neighbors, my family, my co-workers, my enemies, my boss? Let me offer you three biblical ways.

1. Use your life to meet others' needs. When you use your life to meet the needs of other people in a practical way—whether it's taking them a meal, helping them with a project, offering them a ride, praying for them, picking up something at the grocery store, helping them with a plan or a deal—you're ministering to them and showing them love. In 1 Thessalonians 2:8 Paul told the church of Thessalonica that he loved them so much that he gave them not only God's good news, but his life as well.

If you're going to be an ambassador, you must get out of the embassy some of the time. If your whole Christian life is spent inside the four walls of the church, you're not much of an ambassador. Go where people are hurting, where you're needed, where they need love, where they need help and concern. Get out of the embassy and be with people.

2. Show respect to everyone. As an ambassador of Jesus Christ, you are not allowed to be disrespectful to anyone. Why? Because God values every person. It doesn't matter who they are, what they've done, who they've done it to, or how long they've done it—everyone has the dignity of being created in the image of God (Genesis 1:27) and is worthy of respect

The Bible doesn't say to treat everyone you agree with politically with dignity or only those you like. In 1 Peter 2:17 it says, "Show proper respect to everyone, love the family of the believers, fear God, and honor the emperor." It doesn't say respect the government, or emperor in the days of Peter, if you align politically. Maybe you didn't vote for any of the members of the city council. You still need to respect them. Maybe the governor didn't get your vote, but that doesn't mean the governor shouldn't get your respect—that goes for all members of the government, whether it's a mayor, senator, president, etc. The Bible says to respect the government. Why? Because as representatives of Jesus, we are called to show dignity, love, and kindness to everybody.

Let me ask you this. Are ambassadors dogmatic or diplomatic? Diplomatic. They don't stay as ambassadors very long if they're not diplomatic. Dogmatic Christians are not effective ambassadors of Jesus. They may be on the radio. They may be on television. They may write popular books or famous blogs. If they're dogmatic, they may be right, but they're wrong because they're not being diplomatic. The Bible says we're to do everything in love (1 Corinthians 16:14). We're to respect everyone. It doesn't matter who they are or what they've done.

Here's what the Bible says in 1 Peter 3:15: "Always be prepared to give an answer to everyone who asks you to give the reason for the hope that you have. But do this with gentleness and respect." You and I are called to be gentle with everybody and respect everybody. It doesn't matter what they say. It doesn't matter how much they lie about you. It doesn't matter how they accuse you. You are forbidden to hate, forbidden to retaliate, forbidden to attack anyone.

Why? Because you represent Jesus, and Jesus commanded you to turn the other cheek (Matthew 5:39). Jesus said you must overcome evil with good (Romans 12:21). The Bible says that you must bless those who persecute you (Romans 12:14). You are forbidden from using the same tactics used against you or me or anybody else. Why? Because you are an ambassador of Jesus Christ and you are to be known by how you meet others' needs—by loving and respecting everybody.

3. Building bridges. Ambassadors build bridges, not walls. Paul wrote, "Though I am free and belong to no one, I have made myself a slave to everyone, to win as many as possible. To the Jews I became like a Jew, to win the Jews. ... To the weak I became weak, to win the weak. I have become all things to all people so that by all possible means I might save some" (1 Corinthians 9:19–20a, 22). This passage tells us that when dealing with unbelievers, no matter what a person is like, we ought to try to find common ground so we can better share about Christ.

How do you know when you're building a bridge? You get walked on. Count on it. You get trampled. That's what bridges are for. If you never get walked on, then you're not building any bridges. You're only building walls. Walls don't get walked on—bridges get walked on.

Our goal as ambassadors of Jesus is to build bridges of respect and love so that others can walk across to Jesus Christ. We try to find common ground so we can show Christ to all.

What are the rewards of being an ambassador? Colossians 3:23 says that "whatever you do, work at it with all your heart." I don't care what God has called you to do. The Bible says no matter what you do, you should be enthusiastic at it. If you work at Taco Bell, you'd better be enthusiastic about it. If you are a gardener, you'd better do your best. If you do daycare or hospice or if you close multimillion-dollar deals, the Bible says you are to do it with all your heart as though you were working for the

Lord and not for people (Colossians 3:23). Remember that the Lord will reward you with the inheritance He has kept for His people, for Christ is the real Master you serve (Colossians 3:24).

You don't have to like your boss, but you do have to treat your boss with respect and dignity. You don't have to enjoy your neighbors, but you must get along with them. Treat others in such a way to please the Lord and it will produce great rewards in your life.

WORKBOOK

Chapter Six Questions

Question: What is your "disguise"? What roles, jobs, or positions do others think define you? How can you use each of those to be an ambassador for Christ? Do the people with whom you associate in each of these disguises know you represent Jesus? What message is your life giving them about Him?

_____

_____

_____

_____

_____

_____

_____

_____

_____

_____

_____

Question: Are you mission-focused? How is your life becoming more and more about God's mission and less and less about the *stuff* of this world? What are some key distractions that tempt you to get your focus off of your mission and onto trying to create a heaven on earth for yourself? How can you refocus and recommit yourself to God's eternal mission for your life?

_____

_____

_____

_____

_____

_____

_____

_____

_____

_____

Question: What should you do when you fail to show love or when you are a poor representation of Christ? How could you make things right in the following scenarios:

you thoughtlessly spread a rumor about a coworker or neighbor; you get into an argument with a store clerk who was overcharging you; you don't include a relative at a large family get-together because you are not on speaking terms?

_____

_____

_____

_____

_____

_____

_____

_____

_____

_____

Action: Sometimes people do not exercise their authority to speak and their calling to share the message because they are not confident in the message they have been given. Begin equipping yourself with tools that will help you know how to approach various individuals and address their questions about Christ. It is helpful for every believer to know how to share the gospel, speak to basic doctrinal questions, and defend the faith (apologetics).

Remember, the goal is not knowledge for the sake of knowledge or to prove that you are right dogmatically. The goal is to know how to serve them lovingly by meeting them where they are, in all of their doubts and uncertainties about the Lord. Some suggested resources are CARM at https://carm.org and Got Questions at www.gotquestions.org.

Chapter Six Notes

_____

_____

_____

_____

_____

_____

_____

_____

_____

_____

_____

_____

_____

_____

_____

_____

_____

_____

_____

_____

_____

_____

_____

CHAPTER SEVEN

Living a Legacy Life

There's a powerful story that comes out of the Old Testament in 2 Kings 3—a story of three great kingdoms who felt they didn't need God. This story holds three keys to stir your faith.

Let me set it up for you. This was back in the day when Israel was divided into two kingdoms, a northern kingdom and a southern kingdom. Each had a king, and a group of Israelites decided to get the northern king of Israel and the southern king of Judah to join up with the king of Edom and fight a mutual enemy. So, it was to be three to one, stacked odds in favor of the three kingdoms. They didn't need God to show up—or so they thought.

The king of Israel set out with the king of Judah and the king of Edom. After a roundabout march of seven days, the army ran out of water for the soldiers or animals.

"What!" exclaimed the king of Israel. "Has the LORD called us three kings together only to deliver us into the hands of Moab?" But Jehoshaphat asked, "Is there no prophet of the

> LORD here, through whom we may inquire of the LORD?" An officer of the king of Israel answered, "Elisha son of Shaphat is here. He used to pour water on the hands of Elijah." Jehoshaphat said, "The word of the LORD is with him." So the king of Israel and Jehoshaphat and the king of Edom went down to him. Elisha said to the king of Israel, "Why do you want to involve me? Go to the prophets of your father and the prophets of your mother." "No," the king of Israel answered, "because it was the LORD who called us three kings together to deliver us into the hands of Moab." Elisha said, "As surely as the LORD Almighty lives, whom I serve, if I did not have respect for the presence of Jehoshaphat king of Judah, I would not pay any attention to you."
> —*2 Kings 3:10–14*

In other words, he said, "All right, I'm going to help you out, but only because I like Jehoshaphat."

> But now [Elisha said] bring me a harpist. While the harpist was playing, the hand of the LORD came upon Elisha...
> —*2 Kings 3:15*

If you go without God, you wander in the desert without direction. When you worship God, when you turn your eyes upon Him, everything changes. Calling upon God, asking for His presence will bring the hand of the Lord upon you, so you no longer wander alone.

Faith Is Birthed in God's Presence

You may have no faith because you have no presence with Him. Maybe you haven't experienced the presence of God in a long time. Living in the wilderness without Him isn't a place you're safe. Where do you start when you have not heard from God for a long time?

Go seek Him and find Him. He will stir your vision, and your sight will be renewed. That is exactly what Elisha did, and God responded:

> *Thus says the LORD: "Make this valley full of ditches."*
> *—2 Kings 3:16 (NKJV)*

When Elisha sought God, there was no water and there were no clouds in the sky. You might assume the word of the Lord would have been to bring rain, but instead, He said, *"Dig!"* In fact, taking action is another secret to faith.

Faith Has to Go Beyond Inspiration to Participation

In other words, you can't just leave it up to God. If you notice anything about God in the Old and New Testament, He always requires involvement first before the miracles happen. He wants us to move. Jesus took a blind man, laid His hands on him, and then said for the man to go and wash (John 9:7). He could have healed him right there, but He wanted the man to take some steps.

God's commands might seem random. Just do it. God told them to dig some ditches. In the desert. Why were they digging? Because they were putting action to their faith in God's command.

Faith has to go beyond inspiration—it needs a little participation.

For this is what the LORD says: You will see neither wind nor rain, yet this valley will be filled with water...
—2 Kings 3:17–18

But they had to dig. They had to have action.

Faith Continues Regardless of What Is Seen

Some of us haven't seen anything positive in a long time. Some of us are discouraged. Some of us have been praying for something for years, and nothing has happened. Don't give up. Keep digging those ditches. Keep getting close to God, and keep trusting Him. Walk by faith and not by sight (2 Corinthians 5:7). In fact, just close your eyes and stop looking at the circumstances. Turn your eyes on Jesus—just look at Him.

I get discouraged too, but I try to remember that the seen things are temporary and fall out of our lives, but the unseen things are eternal (2 Corinthians 4:18).

You are here for a reason. You are called! You're not here just to suck in air or simply have a good time. You're here to make a difference. And if you're still alive, it's because God's not done with you yet. There are things that He's called you to do, and you have got to get in touch with Him to find out what they are.

A Worthy Calling

I urge you to live a life worthy of the calling you have received.
—Ephesians 4:1

Having a calling is a consistent theme throughout Scripture. When the original manuscripts of the Bible were translated, they didn't have chapter and verse divisions. The translators inserted those so we could more easily find verses and divide topics. But sometimes the separation of chapters causes a loss of continuity. In the original text, it all ran together as one thought. Let me show you the verse before Ephesians 4:1:

> *Now to him who is able to do immeasurably more than all we ask or imagine, according to his power that is at work within us, to him be glory in the church and in Christ Jesus throughout all generations, for ever and ever! Amen. As a prisoner for the Lord, then, I urge you to live a life worthy of the calling you have received.*
> **—Ephesians 3:20–4:1**

I urge you to live a life worthy of the calling that you received. Here's my fear. My fear is that we end up in ordinary living. I want to stir you up to live an extraordinary kind of life. I believe that God has called you to live exceptionally, not because you're extraordinary, but because He is. It's His power at work within you (Ephesians 3:20). But we sometimes choose an ordinary life. This is critical because even Christianity has become boring and mundane, but God wants to move you beyond ordinary in Jesus' name.

Failure does not necessarily mean you don't achieve your goals. Failure, many times, is not having a goal in the first place. You're going to fail, and I'm going to fail if there's nothing to aim for. But why not have a dream, why not have something you're going after?

One of my dreams is that I want to go with all of my kids on their first mission trip. I want to be there when they see a family living in a refrigerator box. I want to be there to witness it with them. That is the life I believe is worthy of my calling.

I believe God has put it inside every one of us to live in an extraordinary kind of way. God never intended you to live an ordinary life. He always intended you to live exceptionally, beyond yourself. He wants you to live a life of transcendence. When you realize a bigger life, it changes everything, not only for you, but also the impact on the people around you.

Create and Protect Your Legacy

How do you create a legacy? Show up and do your best. Go big or go home. Take on extra challenges in the church and at work. Step up your kids' education. Expand your knowledge. Change your career to something challenging that you know is your calling. These efforts offer those around you a chance to watch a legacy grow. When you affect people and people see you doing great things, they are inspired to create their own legacy.

There are a few potential legacy-stoppers, or stuff that can get in the way.

A Wrong View of Self

We often have a poor assessment of self. In other words, we view ourselves inaccurately. Maybe we feel like we're not attractive. We think we aren't productive or skilled. Some people might call this humility, but humility isn't when you think less of yourself—it's when you think of yourself less. Try viewing yourself the way God views you.

God sees greatness in you that you don't see in yourself. And if you'll let Him, Psalm 18:35 (NCV) says He will stoop down and make you great. He essentially says, "If you'll let me, I will stir some of that greatness inside of you. I can see it."

The following are some wrong views you may struggle with:

Insecurity. Some of us are filled with insecurity. We ask, "Who am I?" instead of knowing who we are in Christ. Let the Lord heal you and offer His security. He will make us sure of His love and perfect will if we know our identity is in Him.

Fear. When you fear the unknown and the future, remember that God is in control. Trust Him and let Him work.

Inadequacy. You may be measuring yourself by yourself, rather than by God in you. Without God, you truly are unable to conquer. But with Him, you are more than a conqueror through Him who loved you (Romans 8:37).

Reluctance. You may know you have potential, but you hesitate and are reluctant and procrastinate. No, sign up today. Lead today. Get involved today. Start your legacy now.

In all of these, you have a wrong view of self. Here's what the Bible says about you:

> *But you are a chosen generation, a royal priesthood, a holy nation, His own special people, that you may proclaim the praises of Him who called you out of darkness into His marvelous light...*
>
> **—1 Peter 2:9** *(NKJV)*

If you're going to leave a legacy, you're going to have to have not only a proper view of self, but also of others.

A Wrong View of People

People may bug us. We see them not as people to be loved, but as problems to avoid.

It's your choice how you view people. They can either irritate you or entertain you. For me, I've made a habit of seeing people for their potential, not for their problems. It's a choice. It takes reliance on the Holy Spirit to see the potential in some people. Jesus saw the potential in others and had compassion for them:

> *When [Jesus] saw the crowds, he had compassion on them, because they were harassed and helpless, like sheep without a shepherd.*
>
> **—Matthew 9:36**

His heart broke for them. He had the correct view of people. And you can, too. Love them.

A Wrong View of God

So many times, we forget we serve a miracle-working, powerful, above and beyond, exceedingly, abundantly above anything we can ask for kind of God (Ephesians 3:20). It's easy to forget how awesome our God is. When we should be dreaming God-sized dreams, we're dreaming about what we can attain on our own. I want to challenge you to take your bucket list and give it to God. Ask Him what big dreams He has for you. What does He want you to accomplish?

Challenge yourself. You have to have a few dreams on your bucket list that can only happen if God shows up, because that's where life gets fun. That's the exhilarating, extraordinary life that God intends you to live. I want to live life so big that my dreams can't possibly happen unless God shows up! When you dream big, you pray differently. Life is amazing when we're reliant on God to make our dreams happen.

> *Ah, Sovereign LORD, you have made the heavens and the earth by your great power and outstretched arm. Nothing is too hard for you.*
> **—Jeremiah 32:17**

Pray, "I know You, and You are for me, and that means nothing's too difficult for me, either." Join with God to live a life beyond yourself. Join with God and do something that is impossible. God wants to take you on this exciting journey with Him. Look what Jesus says:

Very truly I tell you, whoever believes in me will do the works I have been doing, and they will do even greater things than these, because I am going to the Father.
                                              —*John 14:12*

I'm calling us all to greater things! I'm calling us to live a life beyond ourselves. I want to challenge you to live a greater things kind of life. I want you to pray for greater things. I want to go on a greater things journey.

But here's the secret—you can't do anything without faith. As long as you live in that realm of what is possible by your own effort, life will be boring! Lifeless! No legacy. It takes faith to be a legacy leaver.

Practical Application

Through faith, we can live lives beyond ourselves, lives that make a difference. Here's how:

Discover the Gifts God Has for You

Chances are, your gifts may not be obvious to you. A spiritual gift is not your natural talent. It's not even your skillset. My spiritual gifts were not obvious to me. At one point in my life, I was afraid to speak to crowds and wasn't a good communicator. But God divinely enabled me to speak and to be comfortable in front of crowds.

What, exactly, is a spiritual gift? A spiritual gift is a divine ability God gives to His children for the purpose of service to Him and others. They are not human talents. Human talents are inadequate to do the work of God. Gifts might relate to administration, hospitality, teaching, or some other area of service.

Do we all have spiritual gifts? Paul said: "We have different gifts, according to the grace given to each of us" (Romans 12:6a).

For instance, my wife, Veronica, is gifted in developing people and teams like no one I've ever seen. She's also got a knack for hospitality that makes others feel genuinely loved—because she does genuinely love people. Like many other Christians, she makes use of her spiritual gifts to serve others in ways that glorify God and build His kingdom.

Others have the divine ability to lead people in worship. It's not enough to have a talented voice or talent with an instrument. You can have musical talent and lack an anointing. It is the divine enablement of God through spiritual gifts that brings anointing to the things we do as service for His Kingdom.

Develop the Gifts God Has Given You

Your gifts change and mature, as you change and mature. For instance, as you first came to Christ, you might have been stirred to something like making coffee and passing out the welcome cards. But now you've matured, you've been at church for a while, and all of a sudden, God is changing you and you see your potential changing. You find a new desire to teach or work on the church lawn or sing.

It's like aging. Our abilities change and mature and allow us to do different things. And that's why you ought to do what the Bible says: "Follow the way of love and eagerly desire the gifts of the Spirit" (1 Corinthians 14:1a). One translation uses the word *covet* in reference to spiritual gifts, "But covet earnestly the best gifts" (1 Corinthians 12:31 KJV). Covet the gifts!

You may know that you have certain gifts, but circumstances have pulled you away from God. No matter what you've done or how far you've gone away from God, He can still use your gifts for His purpose and His plan. Remember, your life is a book. God has written one for every single one of us. I know I've added chapters that God never intended to be in my book, but I'm telling you, when you turn your life over to God, no matter your mistakes, God will always make the final chapters fit.

You may have gotten away from God's purpose for a few chapters, but I'm reminding you of His words, "For this reason I remind you to fan into flame the gift of God, which is in you" (2 Timothy 1:6).

I believe the Holy Spirit is working in you today to get that spark going. It's still in you, and the Spirit of God will make it burn again.

Use the Gifts God Has Given You

Know Jesus. That's what your whole life is about—to go on a discovery of who He is. Listen to me, if you know Jesus, you can summarize your entire life down to this one assignment: to use the gifts God has given you. That's really it.

And none of us are guaranteed time to use our gifts. We need to take every opportunity we have been given to do good (Ephesians 5:16). Because "God has given each of you a gift from his great variety of spiritual gifts. Use them well to serve one another" (1 Peter 4:10 NLT).

I was the sixth of seven kids in my family, bullied in my own home, both physically and emotionally. I was insecure and looking for love and acceptance, and I acted out. I was the guy who always took the dare. "Jason will do it. Just go find Jason, because he'll do anything."

I did all sorts of things to try to make people laugh or endear myself to them. And even after I gave my life to Christ, it was only through revelation that I was able to work on these areas of my heart and mind.

Today, I'm not proud of what I've done or where I've come from. Instead, I'm amazed at what God has done in my life. I always tell people, "If you knew me as I know me, you would fall on your face and worship God right now!" I am a miracle. The man I am today isn't possible with who I am, but I can boldly say that because of the power of God's Holy Spirit inside of me, I am using my gifts for what He had written for me! God did this! God put a passion inside of me to take people on a spiritual journey.

Your Next Steps

If you don't know God as your personal Lord and Savior, and if you're not in love with Him and in a passionate, real relationship with Him, your first step is to *love God*.

Then you need to *love others*. When you are walking in love with your brothers and sisters in Christ, you will find healing, freedom, community, and belonging.

And finally, you need to discover your purpose so you can do what God has called and gifted you to do and so you can *change the world*. You're not on this planet to merely pay bills, get your kids to behave, or go to work on yet another Monday. You have been gifted to make a difference in the world. Whether you're serving on the front lines or behind the scenes, God will equip you to have an impact for Him, one person at a time.

WORKBOOK

Chapter Seven Questions

Question: Describe a God-sized vision that you have for your life. When did God first begin to put this vision in your heart, and how has He continued to confirm and refine the vision? If you have no vision, or you have lost sight of it along the way, how will you be more intentional about getting in His presence and seeking His will?

_____

_____

_____

_____

_____

_____

_____

_____

_____

_____

_____

Question: What are some ways you can dig—that is, participate—in seeing your vision come to life? What are some steps of preparation, planning, or progress you can take? In what ways have you become discouraged or settled into a rut, and how can you renew exceptional living and active faith in the legacy that God desires for you to leave?

_____

_____

_____

_____

_____

_____

_____

_____

_____

_____

Question: Which of these three is the greater obstacle for you—a wrong view of self, of people, or of God? What struggles from your past, problems in your present,

erroneous teaching, or lies from the enemy are causing
you to have this wrong view? Write out the wrong view(s)
that are legacy-stoppers in your life, and for each one give
a scriptural truth with the right view.

_____

_____

_____

_____

_____

_____

_____

_____

_____

_____

Action: Take a spiritual gifts assessment and learn about
the different gifts listed in Scripture. Then, even if you
still aren't sure what your gift is, ask God to give you opportunities to minister to others. By following Him
obediently, you will begin to discover how you are gifted
by Him for service and will begin to understand and develop the vision He has given you for your life.

Chapter Seven Notes

_____

_____

_____

_____

_____

_____

_____

_____

_____

_____

_____

_____

_____

_____

_____

_____

_____

_____

_____

_____

_____

_____

_____

_____

CONCLUSION

Don't Give Up

A man without a vision is a man without a future. And a man without a future will always return to his past.

> *If people can't see what God is doing, they stumble all over themselves; but when they attend to what he reveals, they are most blessed.*
> **—Proverbs 29:18** *(MSG)*

If people can't see what God is doing on the earth or in His church, and if you can't see what God is doing in your life individually, then chaos ensues. Some of you may be convicted that this describes your life.

But when we attend to what God reveals and focus our attention on what He is showing us, then we can more easily recognize our blessings and see how God is working in our lives.

I want that for you. In fact, I can't think of anything I want more for you than for you to live out your dreams and to live your life on purpose.

I want to show you why it's so critically important for you to live out your dreams. Did you know dreams are the language of God? That's how God talks to us.

You might think that you have never heard the audible voice of God, but you have. If you have ever had a God-honoring dream, then you've heard God. That's how He talks. But why does He talk that way? Why doesn't He just talk in English? Why can't I hear it audibly?

God wants to take us outside of realities. God lives outside of the limitations of this earth; He's in a dimension on its own. He's not limited to the laws of gravity, the laws of science, and the laws of earth. So when God wants to speak to us, He often speaks outside of those earthly limitations; He speaks through giving us pictures. Acts 2 says:

> In the last days, God says, I will pour out my Spirit on all people. Your sons and daughters will prophesy, your young men will see visions, your old men will dream dreams.
> —*Acts 2:17*

God says He will intensify the pouring out of His Spirit. His Spirit is already here, but He will pour it out in the last days for all people so that your sons and daughters, young men and women, and old men and women will prophesy, see visions, and experience dreams, respectively.

Notice all three of these—prophecies, visions, and dreams—are pictures of things that have not happened yet. God wants you to navigate through the generation we live in. God has to give us the picture before He can fulfill it. According to this verse in Acts, God's purpose in touching the earth during the last days is to give us these visions, pictures, and dreams. Though nobody knows for sure, I believe we're living in the last days right now, so this message is mission critical and especially relevant.

Dreams are the language of the Spirit. I maintain God is trying to speak to us, show us things, and reveal Himself to us, and we need to tune in to God. My goal in this chapter is not just to stir you inside, but to help you hear from God and know He speaks to you, so that you can get a dream from Him.

And for a lot of people, it's not that they don't dream; they've just become convinced the dream can never happen for them. Well, let me just tell you a truth about that— dreams are conceived long before they're achieved. There's always space between the promise and the fulfillment. I want to encourage you and build your faith while you're in that space. He's the Alpha and the Omega, the Beginning and the End (Revelation 22:13), but we're here living in the middle of the dream.

What do you do? Well, you can't talk about this without talking about Joseph. If you're new to the Bible, it's one of the oldest stories, found in the book of Genesis (chapters 37–50).

Joseph was the eleventh of twelve kids in the family, and he was favored by his father. Understandably, his older brothers resented him and were jealous.

Joseph was also a dreamer. In fact, the Bible says this about him:

Joseph had a dream, and when he told it to his brothers,

they hated him all the more. He said to them, "Listen to this dream I had: We were binding sheaves of grain out in the field when suddenly my sheaf rose and stood upright, while your sheaves gathered around mine and bowed down to it."

—Genesis 37:5–7

Joseph boldly told his brothers they would someday bow down to him. Can you imagine how much that stirred their jealousy?

We see from this example why God doesn't give us dreams and fulfill them right away. We can see from Joseph's attitude that he's prideful and not ready and still in need of some real character development.

God has big dreams for you, just as He did for Joseph—and He will persevere as He seeks to get rid of anything that stands in the way. God may have given you a big dream and revealed a big destiny in His plans for you. But if you become prideful about it, you won't be able to step into that destiny. That's why there's a space—a distance—because God works inside of us in the process.

Joseph's brothers weren't too excited about his dream, and they said:

"Here comes that dreamer!" they said to each other. "Come now, let's kill him and let's throw him into one of these cisterns and say that a ferocious animal devoured him. Then we'll see what comes of his dreams."

—Genesis 37:19–20

Joseph's brothers mocked him, and many of us have also experienced being mocked. Thankfully, most of us have not experienced family members or friends actually plotting to physically harm us. Most of us, however, can probably relate to being scorned or made fun of, and we can look back at Joseph as an example.

Don't Give Up on the Dream

Let's focus on a few truths we can learn from Joseph's story in the Bible. The first lesson is not to give up on your dream.

1. Don't Give Up on Your Dream—Even If It Doesn't Start Well

A lot of us have had seemingly unattainable dreams, yet we've claimed God's promises and believed in God's ability to work through us. And then, history happens— events or things take place and convince us that we are now disqualified and that God can no longer work through us. Some stumble from the start and think that past or current sins equate to being unfit to be used by God, but don't believe that lie.

The enemy's job is to convince you that you're disqualified. But God has a history, a track record, of using people with checkered pasts to do great things. If you look at the characters of the Bible, they're just that—characters. They had issues—big issues! And God intentionally used them to show us He can use anyone.

God chose Paul, and God chose Peter. You wouldn't have chosen them and I wouldn't have chosen them, but God knowingly chose them and used them to do great things, despite their sins and problematic situations. I love this verse:

> I thank Christ Jesus our Lord, who has given me strength, that he considered me trustworthy, appointing me to his service. Even though I was once a blasphemer and a perse-cutor and a violent man, I was shown mercy because I acted in ignorance and unbelief.
> —1 Timothy 1:12–13

Paul was amazed that God looked down and saw him in his mess and still chose him, considering him faithful to carry out His message.

I don't know what you've been through or what you've done, but God's dream for your life can still come to pass. Don't measure your dream by who you think you are or how long you've stayed in that pit; measure it by who your God is. And don't give up!

2. Don't Give Up on Your Dream—Even If the Journey Is Full of Surprises

The journey is going to be full of surprises. And chances are, there will be twice as many bad days as good days. Let us look again to Joseph's example and see how he handled the dreadful surprises he encountered:

- *Slavery.* Joseph's brothers were originally going to kill him, but thought better of it and instead sold him into slavery. It did not appear that any dreams Joseph had for his life would be possible. But once in Potiphar's house, it became apparent that God's hand was on Joseph's life and he was given favor and promoted to chief of staff Joseph persevered in his situation and it paid off. Would you have given up or gone on?

- *False accusation.* Potiphar's wife wanted to have sex with Joseph, but he rejected her and was faithful to his employer—her husband. She continued trying to entice him until he ran away. Joseph acted with integrity, yet she falsely accused him to Potiphar of trying to rape her. Did he give up or go on?

- *Prison.* Potiphar threw Joseph into prison for assaulting his wife. These prisons weren't like the ones we have today. They were underground dungeons with abhorrent living situations. But did Joseph give up or go on? He acted in such a manner to win favor of the warden.

- *Forgotten.* While still in custody, Joseph was made attendant to two of Pharaoh's officials, the chief cupbearer and the baker, who were also in prison. Joseph interpreted their dreams and asked that they remember him upon their release and request his release from Pharaoh. But they would not remember him for two more years. Did Joseph give up or go on?

When the chief cup bearer eventually did remember Joseph, he interpreted Pharaoh's dreams and was made second in command. Joseph persisted and realized God's dreams for his life.

And we know that in all things God works for the good of those who love him, who have been called according to his purpose.

—**Romans 8:28**

When Paul says "all things," that means your current situation, your current marriage, your current employer, your current financial outlook, your current health, etc. You need to know God is at work in all things because He calls us for His purpose.

Here's one more. Don't give up on your dreams.

3. Don't Give Up on Your Dream—Even If It Takes a Long Time to Realize

It will take a long time to see your dreams come to fruition. I wanted to write this book to encourage you to welcome a new season of believing God for greater things, even when it feels like they can't happen. Don't lose patience in His plans:

These things I plan won't happen right away. Slowly, steadily, surely, the time approaches when the vision will be fulfilled. If it seems slow, do not despair, for these things will surely come to pass. Just be patient! They will not be overdue a single day!

—**Habakkuk 2:3** *(TLB)*

I don't know about you, but I don't like the word

patient. God's purpose and plan for you will not be overdue by a single day. We live in a society where we're used
to things in an instant. We want hot 'n ready; that might
work if you want real cheap pizza, but it doesn't work if
you're following God. God works slow and steady.

That's why Galatians says:

> *Let us not become weary in doing good, for at the proper
> time we will reap a harvest if we do not give up.*
> **—Galatians 6:9**

Along the Way

Do not give up! I know that's easier said than done. I
have three principles I live by that have helped me to keep
going and that have saved my life in more ways than you
can possibly imagine.

1. Recognize and value the process.

Why? Because God does. When something is happening *to* you, God wants to do something *in* you. That's a
fact, and it's not necessarily the part of the journey we enjoy, but it is best for us. God doesn't bring trouble, but
He'll use it.

You might be thinking, "Oh, God, rescue me from this
trial." God may be saying, "I will! But let's learn something first. Let's work through this a little bit."

We pray, "God, take it away, take it away!" But we
need to change our prayer to, "Lord, what are You trying
to teach me in this?" If you do that, I promise you, you'll

get out of it faster than just asking God to take it away. God loves working on our character; He's not interested in working for your comfort. He wants to use you in ways you could never possibly imagine. It's like when my kids wake up in the morning and say, "I don't want to go to school!" I'm not interested in their comfort! I'm interested in developing them more, and I certainly don't say, "Ok, just sleep in." No way!

God's interested in developing you, but if you don't recognize and value the process, your road through life will be a bummer. On the other hand, if you lean into God, the journey is so much better. Life is not what happens to you—it's how you respond to things, which, in turn, leads God and others to respond. If you respond correctly, God can work amazing things through your trials:

> *So be truly glad. There is wonderful joy ahead, even though you have to endure many trials for a little while. These trials will show that your faith is genuine. It is being tested as fire tests and purifies gold...*
> **—1 Peter 1:6–7** *(NLT)*

The process for making pure gold is fascinating. It's heated to an extreme temperature, which results in the impurities rising to the top for skimming. We don't realize it, but God has us in a skimming process. So often, we try to pray away the very fire He's using to purify us!

Every test in life is a teachable lesson to God. Every experience is an education. God can use everything. Keep your faith strong through many trials, and it will bring you much praise, glory, and honor on the day when Jesus Christ is revealed to the whole world:

Consider it pure joy, my brothers, whenever you face trials of many kinds, because you know that the testing of your faith develops perseverance.

—James 1:2–3

I have yet to meet the person who is joyful over trials. "I'm going through a trial! It's awesome!" Nobody does that. I'm trying to help you get a little perspective of what God is doing through your trial.

In the next verse, James continues that our trials make us "mature and complete, not lacking anything." I don't want to lack anything, so that sounds a bit more palatable.

If we don't learn this principle, life becomes miserable. But when we start recognizing, "*Ohhh!* That's what that's all about! Teach me, Lord, and develop me," then we'll more easily walk through these trials and tests of life.

2. Refuse to let offenses stop you.

Offenses are coming your way. Some people seem as if their calling in life is to destroy yours. Yes, there are people like that, and if you don't forgive them every day, resentment will creep in and ultimately be a dream killer. It will stop you dead in your tracks, probably more than anything else.

Think of Joseph, who was sold by his own brothers. He did not let resentment stop his dreams. When he had the chance to get revenge, he forgave. Because of the famine in the land, Joseph's brothers traveled to Egypt to get food. But guess who was in charge of the food distribution? The Lord had directed Joseph to store up grain, and he oversaw its distribution. His brothers didn't recognize him, and they bowed before him just as Joseph had predicted from his dream when he was seventeen.

It seems that would have been the moment when Joseph said, "I curse thee, and I send thee to go build a pyramid. May the flies of a thousand camels find your armpits!"

This was his chance. He could do it—but he didn't. Instead, he told them he was their brother Joseph. And this is my favorite verse from Joseph's story: "You intended to harm me, but God intended it for good" (Genesis 50:20).

Here we see a beautiful picture of forgiving upon indescribable harm. Joseph was gracious and moved on. It's a powerful example of how we should respond when others do us harm.

Jesus warned us about offenses: "Then He said to the disciples, 'It is impossible that no offenses should come'" (Luke 17:1 NKJV). You can't avoid them. Offenses are going to happen. Here's what Paul said about the offenses we face:

> *For our struggle is not against flesh and blood, but against the rulers, against the authorities, against the powers of this dark world and against the spiritual forces of evil in the heavenly realms.*
> **—Ephesians 6:12**

Paul explains our struggle is not against the person who hates us or hurts us. We have a real enemy; it's the devil and his forces. Once we understand we are in a spiritual battle and it's the devil behind the people who come at us, then it is easier for us to step back and forgive our offenders and show them love.

Jesus knew such things would happen, and He knew where the struggle would come from. He even encouraged us to ask for God's forgiveness as we forgive others. I pray that often, because resentment is a dream killer. When we put the offenses in perspective, we can move forward in our dreams.

3. Remember, God is always with you.

He is *always* with you. On the day Joseph was sold into slavery—his worst day ever—God was with him "so that he prospered" (Genesis 39:2)!

And when Joseph ended up in prison, the Bible says he was not alone: "…the LORD was with him; he showed him kindness and granted him favor" (Genesis 39:20–21).

Psalm 139 says:

> *If I go up to the heavens, you are there; if I make my bed in the depths, you are there. If I rise on the wings of the dawn, if I settle on the far side of the sea, even there your hand will guide me, your right hand will hold me fast.*
> **—Psalm 139:8–10**

We can find hope and strength in God:

> *God is our refuge and strength, an ever-present help in trouble.*
> **—Psalm 46:1**

When you pass through the waters, I will be with you; and when you pass through the rivers, they will not sweep over you. When you walk through the fire, you will not be burned; the flames will not set you ablaze. ... Do not be afraid, for I am with you...
—Isaiah 43:2, 5

"Do not be afraid of them, for I am with you and will rescue you," declares the LORD.
—Jeremiah 1:8

"They will fight against you but will not overcome you, for I am with you and will rescue you," declares the LORD.
—Jeremiah 1:19

And one of the last words out of Jesus' mouth was:

...and teaching them to obey everything I have commanded you. And surely I am with you always, to the very end of the age."
—Matthew 28:20

How comforting it is to know that no matter what we go through along life's way, God is always there with us and developing us for His plans. Use Him as your strength and know that He wants better for you.

Don't give up the dreams! Love God, love others, and let God show you what He has for you. His plan for your life is greater. His plan for your life is better than your plan.

About the Author

Jason Hanash is the founding Pastor of Discovery Church, one of the fastest-growing churches in America. He also established the Discovery Church Network—a church planting multiplication network of leaders and churches. Jason is a speaker, author, leadership coach, and church-planting coach.

About Sermon To Book

SermonToBook.com began with a simple belief: that sermons should be touching lives, *not* collecting dust. That's why we turn sermons into high-quality books that are accessible to people all over the globe.

Turning your sermon series into a book exposes more people to God's Word, better equips you for counseling, accelerates future sermon prep, adds credibility to your ministry, and even helps make ends meet during tight times.

John 21:25 tells us that the world itself couldn't contain the books that would be written about the work of Jesus Christ. Our mission is to try anyway. Because in heaven, there will no longer be a need for sermons or books. Our time is now.

If God so leads you, we'd love to work with you on your sermon or sermon series.

Visit www.sermontobook.com to learn more.

REFERENCES

Notes

[1] Pascal, Blaise. *Pensées*. Dover Publications, 2003, p. 113.

[2] Hodges, Chris. *The Daniel Dilemma: How to Stand Firm and Live Well in a Culture of Compromise*. Thomas Nelson, 2017.

[3] Duguid, Iain M. and Paul D. Wegner. "Introduction to Daniel." *ESV Study Bible*. Crossway, 2008, p. 1581.

[4] Strong, James. "H1840 – Daniye'l." In *Strong's Exhaustive Concordance of the Bible*. Hunt & Eaton, 1894. Quoted in Blue Letter Bible. https://www.blueletterbible.org/lang/lexicon/lexicon.cfm?t=kjv&strongs=h1840.

[5] "The Daniel of the Book of Daniel." In *Lexham Bible Dictionary*, edited by John D. Barry. Lexham Press, 2016.

[6] Strong, James. "H2608 – Chananyah." In *Strong's Exhaustive Concordance of the Bible*. Hunt & Eaton, 1894. Quoted in Blue Letter Bible. https://www.blueletterbible.org/lang/lexicon/lexicon.cfm?Strongs=H2608&t=KJV.

[7] Carpenter, EuGene and David Thompson. "Daniel 1:3–7." In

Cornerstone Biblical Commentary: Ezekiel, Daniel. Tyndale House, 2018, p. 318.

[8] Carpenter and Thompson, "Daniel 1:3–7."

[9] Hodges, *The Daniel Dilemma*, p. 8.

[10] Hodges, *The Daniel Dilemma*, p. 9.

[11] Hodges, *The Daniel Dilemma*, p. 9.

[12] Gathercole, Simon J. "Introduction to Galatians." *ESV Study Bible.* Crossway, 2008, p. 2240.

[13] Elie, Tom. "The 2 Questions God Will Ask at the Pearly Gates." *Oasis World Ministries.* https://myemail.constantcontact.com/The-2-Questions-God-Will-Ask-at-the-Pearly-Gates---ONE-MINUTE-WITNESS.html?soid=1101917508491&aid=RoS-ytUQ8kY.

[14] Evans, Tony. *Tony Evans' Book of Illustrations: Stories, Quotes, and Anecdotes from More than 30 Years of Preaching and Public Speaking.* Moody Publishers, 2009.

[15] Lewis, C.S. *C.S. Lewis: Readings for Meditation and Reflection.* Harper Collins, 1996.

[16] "Alumni Association News." *UCLA Monthly.* March-April 1981, p. 1. Cited in John Trent and Gary Smalley, *The Blessing* (Thomas Nelson, 2011).

Made in the USA
Middletown, DE
18 July 2021